What I Saw

Sailing in the California Delta

Jackie Philpott

Claire

You are always in my heart

CONTENTS

INTRODUCTION

In the spring of 2017 I decided to write a book about sailing in the Delta. After all, I had a sailboat and I thought I knew how to get there. After sailing across San Pablo Bay I would continue under the Carquinez Bridge. I would find the Delta somewhere on the other side of that vast, murky body of water that I could see from my car as I drove across the bridge. Right?

First I needed a **How to get to the Delta on your Sailboat** guide. Except that I couldn't find one. Nuthin. Oh, there were stories in Latitude 38 about the Delta Ditch Run race, with photos of wild eyed sailors hanging on as their spinnakers slow drag raced them through the Carquinez Strait and beyond. There were whole sections in Latitude devoted to the Delta Doo Dah, with photos of people jumping into brown water and laying around looking silly on flotation toys that were too small for them. It did look like fun, but – again - how did one actually get there?

I decided to look for cheap paperback guidebooks. You know, like this one. The kind you read and leave at the harbormaster's table or forget in a corner of your boat until it gets moldy. But I couldn't find any of those, either. The only books I found were published in 1964 and 1976 and 1983. They were hardbound books written by serious people. They wrote about the Delta's history and its people and its culture, for crying out loud. This was not what I was looking for. I just wanted that How To Get There paperback. But I did read them. Because, why not? It was background research.

What struck me about the legitimate published books I found were the photos of people from half a century ago. They were jumping into the brown water and laying around looking silly on flotation toys that were too small for them. Seriously? This intrigued me. I decided that maybe there is something about the Delta that causes people to become happy: Maybe something in that water. I had heard that people still go to the Delta to be happy and silly. Could that be possible fifty and sixty years later? And if they do, how do they get there? I decided that it was up to me to sail there and report back.

The title of this book is **What I Saw: Sailing in the California Delta**. Truth be told, my boat and I were lost a good portion of the four summers we spent there. However, there is a difference between not knowing where you are and being lost. Let me explain.

Since I had never been to the Delta, I decided to first drive there in my car. Like a scout in those old cowboy movies, I would reconnoiter, see if the natives were friendly. My plan seemed prudent to me at the time. I had a general idea of how to get there, and besides, if I needed it there was a map of California in the glove compartment. So on May 30, 2017 I drove from Oakland toward the Delta. Somehow I found my way to the Antioch Bridge, which I crossed.

As I descended the Antioch Bridge the flat verdant land lay before me like another world. So different, so lush and rural compared to the city I had left behind. At the bottom of the bridge I pulled over to the side of Highway 160 and dug around for my map. Where was I going? I had no idea. I was going to the Delta.

I reached into the glove compartment and found an outdated AAA map of California. I perused it. On one side was the overall map of California from Brookings, Oregon to Tijuana, Mexico and everything in between. The whole of the Delta was represented in a very small space less than 4 square inches.

Surely on the other side there would be an enlarged insert of the Delta? Well, no. There wasn't. There were inserts for Sacramento, San Francisco, San Diego, Yosemite Valley and Monterey Peninsula. There was an insert for Palm Springs and the Napa/Sonoma Valleys, Sequoia, Lassen and Kings Canyon National parks and Lake Tahoe. There was even an insert dedicated to the LA Freeway system. There was no insert for the Delta.

I popped the trunk, dug around in my sailing bag and found a laminated map of Delta waterways. For about an hour I tried to use it, but it wasn't meant for a car. It was meant for a shallow draft fishing boat and proved totally useless to me on the narrow levee roads of the Delta. My first turn onto Twitchell Island Road led me around what I later learned was the Delta loop, which led in turn to Oxbow Marina. How did I get from one place to the other? I have no idea.

For lunch I stopped in the river town of Rio Vista. Parking near the city boat launch, I walked up a block or so to Main Street and ate at the Rio Vista Bakery and café. Run by a mother together with her young son behind the cash register, there were colorful cotton tablecloths and small vases with flowers on each small table. In addition to sandwiches and

salads there were pastries, lattes, espressos and just plain ordinary coffee or tea. They also serve Dreyers ice cream any time of the day.

I drove and I drove and I drove. I was hopelessly lost for hours. To my city eyes, everything was new and lovely. There was water everywhere, people were sitting in folding chairs and fishing alongside the road, around the next corner there were miles of beautifully maintained orchards. Small new trees with their little legs wrapped in white like race horses, carefully trimmed mature trees, green alfalfa fields and then herds of cattle, goats and ... llamas! Everything seemed so different to me, so unique.

Stopping often to walk around, I got closer to rivers and sloughs. I walked across bridges and listened to the country sounds of birds, trees, tractors, motorboats and water. So many different water sounds! Sluggish in some of the sloughs, faster as it moved underneath the bridges.

Beautiful rows of fruit trees grew below the road to starboard, and the old Sacramento River came into and out of sight to port. Not knowing enough to turn off Highway 160 at Walnut Grove, I kept driving all the way to Cortland: the Bartlett Pear Capital of the World. Where was I headed? I had no idea and I didn't mind at all.

Late in the afternoon, as I drove home, the mighty Sacramento River was very impressive. There was big wind that day, and its currents were obviously powerful, the whitecaps one on top of each other as they raced down toward the ocean. My experience driving around that first day was, metaphorically, a perfect introduction. Because the remarkable California Delta I found isn't on any map.

FIRST THINGS FIRST

Here are some things I've learned from singlehanding in the Delta:

- If you are a person who likes backpacking you are more likely to enjoy sailing in the Delta than if you prefer staying in a hotel with room service.
- If you get antsy when you don't have something to do with your hands or someone to talk with, then single handing in the Delta might not be your cup of tea.
- If you have heard: "The rivers and sloughs are too narrow to sail," you have talked to someone who has never sailed in the Delta.
- If you have heard: "The rivers and sloughs are too shallow to sail," you are talking to another person who has never sailed in the Delta.
- Phone reception in the Delta is better than most places on the water in the San Francisco Bay.
- You can read a lot of books in the Delta, especially if you're anchored and alone on your sailboat where no one can find you. If you like to read the Delta may become your happy place.

CERTAINTIES THAT MUST BE ADDRESSED:

- It will be hot in June, July and August. Come prepared.
- Yes, there will be bugs, though not as many as in the Amazon and mostly just before the sun goes down.
- It is best to eat your chocolate with breakfast because it will melt before noon.
- You will need a chart plotter. They're cheap. Don't leave home without one. I use MX Mariner with NOAA Chart Region 14 downloaded. It cost $6.99 in 2013 and I've loaded it onto several different inexpensive android tablets since then.
- Delta wind is similar to wind in the San Francisco Bay insofar as there is less in the morning, more in the afternoon.

• If your engine is cooled with raw water: when you get stuck in the mud (and you will get stuck in the mud) don't turn on the engine! Rock your boat, kedge, call a friend or Boat US. You don't want that mud sucked up into your engine. Don't ask me how I know this.

How do you get to the Delta of your dreams? Some people prefer to motor there so they have more time to lay around like slugs. Other people time their trip so they can sail the whole way on a flood current. Simply put, first you sail under the Carquinez Bridge, then continue on until you sail under the Benicia-Martinez Bridge. You know that vast expanse of water you see when you are the passenger in a car driving over either of those bridges? That's where you will be sailing. You say you never see any sailboats down there? That's what I'm talking about! You will look so tiny to all those drivers up there! They will ask themselves:

"Where is that sailboat going?"

And you? On your sailboat? You will be the one going off on the adventure. They will be driving to Fairfield or Sacramento or Redding. So mundane.

What about those wicked fast currents? Sail with the ebb or with the flood? Excellent questions. Use your head and make your own decisions. Read the tide book carefully. Think about it: On your way up to the Delta, do you want to arrive at the Carquinez Bridge at maximum ebb tide? Probably not a good idea. Returning from the Delta, consider this: Does your boat have an engine? If you don't have an engine you'll have to tack a lot coming back. An awful lot.

ABOUT DURA MATER

Dura Mater is a 1979 Cal 2-27, built by Jensen Marine in Costa Mesa, California. Her Engine by Dave (Morris) is an 11 horsepower, two cylinder diesel Universal M-15. Except for entering and exiting marinas, during our first three years in the Delta I was able to sail almost everywhere.

All stories in this book assume that the reader understands Dura Mater is no race boat and your mileage may vary. She weighs 6700 before safety equipment, her skipper or all chocolate aboard. Again, except when so noted, all trips were under sail. I bought two used spinnakers for $120/each and Bob Johnston sold me an aluminum spinnaker pole for a pittance that is the perfect size for me to dip gybe: it is ½ inch shorter than DM's J measurement of 12 feet.

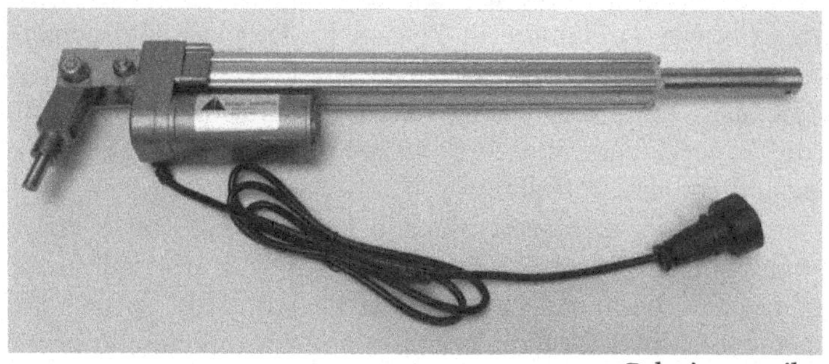

Pelagic autopilot

Brian Boschma installed one of his Pelagic autopilots way back when they were prototypes and it has worked perfectly ever since.

For cooking I use a butane single burner camp stove. Recommended by Ichiro Yamawaki, it cost $12.99 at the Ranch Market in El Cerrito where four small canisters of butane sell for $6.99.

DM also has that crucial bit of Delta equipment: a depth finder. The Humminbird fish finder supposedly measures depth up to 200 feet, but it measured 450' deep off the coast of Cape San Martin, so that's a testament to its expansive abilities. It does a remarkable job in the Delta sloughs, and when it reads five feet I know to tack away quickly.

And finally, right after I bought Dura Mater in 2012 I took a jigsaw to all the stinky hoses that led to the head, removed the porcelain toilet and installed a porta-pottie. It works for me, though you might prefer something else. Something more civilized, maybe?

Dura Mater has never been up the Delta, so up we go. Don't know why it's called "Up the Delta", when the sailing is downwind, but that's the way it is. What does this mean? I have no idea. But I'm going up the Delta to find out. And I'm taking my tape recorder and camera with me.

What to bring? Dave Morris suggests, "a bikini, tequila, mosquito repellent, sunscreen." He also told me to change my transmission fluid before I go, which I can do because he showed me how. And I'm taking three impellers because I have heard that the tule weed gums them up.

Bob Johnston tells me: "You'll want bug screens for your companionway". I see a bug pattern here. So I called my friend Stacey LaFlamme in Wisconsin. People in Wisconsin know bugs. I asked her if citronella candles work. People from Wisconsin have very nice social skills. Stacey hedged and said, "I never had much luck with citronella." In Wisconsin-speak that means, "Hell no!"

According to Stacey, Skin So Soft oil spray by Avon is what works to stave off mosquitoes. I was worried for a nanosecond because I haven't seen an Avon lady in Oakland in forever. But I do have a laptop and I know how to type: EBAY. And there it was! Two spray bottles. In case I meet up with a lot of those little buggers. For $8 each. So I typed in my credit card and they arrived two days later, free shipping. Thank you, EBAY.

I also have some mosquito netting, known as "tulle" in the fabric trade, which I bought for some long abandoned ballet tutu costume. It has silver stars embedded in it. I have yards of it, and I'll tape it to my single hatch and companionway entrance with narrow strips of sticky-back Velcro.

SUMMER ONE 2017

Berkeley Marina to Benicia Marina
9:45 am – 3:15 pm = 5.5 hours, 29 nm.

7.2.17 I gave up my slip in Berkeley Marina because I didn't know how long I would be gone. There was a lot of wind on the Olympic Circle that early in the morning, and DM was going 7+ knots upwind. That's a lot for DM going downwind, so I was impressed by her fortitude. My boat. She's a tank. And that was before we got into the San Pablo Bay. There was lots of wind in San Pablo Bay and we surfed across it double reefed. Max speed 7.7 knots between Berkeley and Red Rock.

I had done the Singlehanded Sailing Society's Vallejo 1-2 race every year since 2009, but that race is always in the fall. I had never before experienced the San Pablo Bay in its glory. But that there is a long fetch, and the waves got big. Whooee!

Dura Mater at Benicia Marina

Holy Cow! We surfed with the flood for awhile and then we surfed without it, and we got to the Benicia Marina in 5.5 hours.

Now, people who do the Delta Ditch Run in those fancy race boats with crew might say, “Big deal! We fly by that marina carrying spinnakers at 20 knots.” Yes, well, those of us with old fat boats go slower and maybe we are more easily impressed.

Bob J also told me to call ahead for a slip, but I forgot. Instead I called from the middle of San Pablo Bay. Alec in the Benicia harbormaster’s office told me that usually people reserve slips for that weekend a year in advance. I whined a little and Alec gave me one anyway. I promised to leave early the next day, before all the big cabin cruisers were due. The Benicia Marina was only $20 for the night. What a great deal. Thank you, Alec.

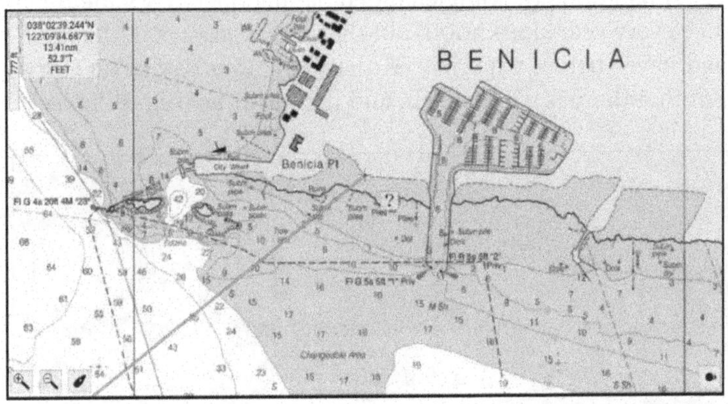

The next morning I was ready early to leave with the water. Last year at Drakes Bay Chris Case showed off the French press his wife Joni bought him for his boat, FUGU. I ran right out and bought one of my own, and it does not disappoint. Whew! Drinking Medaglio espresso made in my own French press really wakes me up. And then I was ready to roll, onward to The Delta.

Benicia Marina to Owl Harbor 10:15 am – 3:15 pm, 31.3 nm, 5.7 knots average downwind in flood.
Max speed = 8.5 knots.

7.3.17 This is our first time in the Delta. I'd like to arrive in early afternoon and we need to establish a base camp. So onward we go, under the Carquinez Bridge, through Carquinez Strait, then under the Benicia-Martinez Bridge. It's a bit of a slog along the Bulls Head Channel, which cuts through the southern edge of Suisun Bay, but there are channel markers all along the way, each within sight as we approach them in numeric order. Remember the phrase "Red Right Returning" and it's a cakewalk.

If you're sailing on the Fourth of July weekend, just follow the boats with toys on their cabin tops. Stay in the deep water of the channel, on to Preston Point Reach, Roe Island Channel and finally to Port Chicago Reach. This is "where wind lives", according to Steve Cameron, a sailor and wind surfer who spends a good deal of time in the Delta.

Once you sail past Middle Ground and Chipps Island, both to port, it's time to start thinking about whether you want to enter the Delta via the San Joaquin River or the Sacramento. If you turn to starboard at R "30" you will head southeast into New York Slough. This leads to the San Joaquin. If you decide instead to go northeast, that will take you up the Sacramento's deep water shipping channel. You get to decide yourself. Isn't that fun? Like an unsupervised child.

Dura Mater and I turn to starboard at R "30", and then the numbers start all over again. The new numbers start on port side with G.R."NY" G6s. What does this mean? Well, I only know because I looked it up. It is the first channel marker for New York Slough, the waterway that leads southeast. It is green and red, hence the GR. And what is a slough? Lots of definitions for that word, including "an area of soft muddy ground; swamp or swamplike region". Huh. Whatever it is, DM and I were in it, along for the flood ride.

Immediately after we turned to starboard there was the Pittsburg Yacht Club, and beyond that a long stretch of water all the way to the Antioch Bridge, visible in the distance.

Once we turned from Suisun Bay into the New York Slough we entered a different world. I raised the spinnaker, set the Pelagic and just sat back and watched. To our starboard side everything was industrial while on the portside everything was ... Delta.

Every color green you can imagine, lush and low to the water, leaning with the wind against a cobalt blue sky. It was stunningly beautiful. Except for the occasional low hum of some kind of generators along the shoreline, the only sounds were, increasingly, of birds and more birds and the whooshing of water against DM's hull. It was very calming, an idyllic experience: a gentle spinnaker run on a flood tide from Benicia all the way to Owl Harbor in Isleton. I couldn't stop taking photos, to remember my experience, to share it. Really, I was smitten.

Abandoned dredger at entrance to Seven Mile Slough

If you are going to Owl Harbor, keep going until you see G 41, then turn to port at the decrepit dredger.

Voila!

Owl Harbor view from Dura Mater

We are now in Seven Mile Slough, at the end of which is Owl Harbor. We arrive at our slip on J Dock and admire the view from Dura Mater's cockpit.

7.4.17 Up with the sun in Owl Harbor, awake with the dueling roosters. It's chilly enough for me to wish I hadn't taken all my San Francisco Bay wool caps out of the clothes net. I am learning what I need while living aboard.

For example, re-fillable bottled water. Lots of bottles, full of lots of water. I'm also learning what I don't need to bring: garlic. There is a community garden here with vegetables and two types of garlic. There are dozens of chickens and beautiful small eggs pressed upon me by the generous manager of the marina, Devery. Scrambled eggs with sauteed red onions and Havarti cheese until the cheese is gone.

As I'm washing up the dishes I hear the drone of a crop duster flying over the fields nearby. Hay fields, fruit fields, corn fields laid out in perfect lines by driverless tractors that probably have Kubota engines similar to the one in Dura Mater. I'm sure they don't run any better than her Engine by Dave.

I am getting acclimated to The Delta. It is too hot to stand barefoot on the fiberglass of Dura Mater's cockpit, so this is what you do in The Delta: you jump in the water. It's wonderfully refreshing. Then you go lay down and take a nap. Bug screens can wait. Wake up after awhile, then jump into the water again. Read a book. Think about doing some work. Jump in the water instead. 92 degrees is hot. Paddle around, then sit under an umbrella for awhile. Repeat. Chat with your neighbors and get to know all the dogs on the dock. Repeat until dinner time: couscous, garlic, red onion in olive oil with garlic powder. Add any kind of cheese, in this case, Havarti, then eat.

Couscous is good because you don't waste any water. After cooking noodles you drain the water out. Water is precious, don't you know? This is California. Don't waste water boiling it for noodles, then drain it out. Make couscous instead. Boil the water, put some olive oil or butter in it, stir in the couscous, then cover it. All done. You'll get used to the taste.

That was a long day in the sun. I'm tired and very sweaty, even after all that jumping in the water. Owl Harbor has very nice showers. Nicer than a lot of yacht clubs. And there are bicycles for visitors to use, especially useful for those of us way down the levee (another new word) on J Dock. So I took a bike ride up to the showers and when I was nice and clean I sprayed myself ALL over with Skin So Soft by Avon.

Everywhere. Because mosquitoes love my blood. You say they love your blood? Well, it's not a competition, but they love mine more.

Now it's time for bed. I settle in, smug in the knowledge that I am covered in Skin So Soft by Avon. I lay down in the VBerth, start to read a book, and that's when I hear the crop duster again. At night? Huh? Then I see it. A mosquito so big it looks like a small lizard. Up on the headliner. Waiting. Bad language erupts and then I remember the "tulle" (so many new words today). I get up and retrieve the fly swatter Synthia gave me back in 2015 when we were all rafted up in Drakes Bay.

I smack that lizard-bug hard. There is blood everywhere. Dark red blood. It must be mine, because ... as has been said,

"I'm the only one here".

Then I get out the green frog tape and tape the tulle over my hatch and companionway. A thin layer of ballerina tutu material embedded with silver stars now protects me from those monster mosquitoes out there. The temperature drops from the daytime high of 92 to 56 degrees during the night. Seriously.

In the Delta the only sounds at night are the far away rumble of a real freight train in the distance, a bullfrog once in awhile and maybe the gentle whine of a Delta Lizard-Bug. I close my eyes and sleep like a lizard my first night in the Delta.

ALL SLOUGHS LEAD TO OWL HARBOR

On my second morning at Owl Harbor I walk the length of the marina property, up along the levee road that runs from the gated entrance to its other end.

Looking down, I watch as a woman pulls a wagon along the road between the alfalfa fields and the marina. She walks slowly, waiting patiently for two very slow older dogs. Later I will learn that it is Devery Stockon.

She pulls the wagon along the wide dirt road, lined with huge old pink and white oleander bushes grown twenty feet high, trimmed as trees now, offering shade or not, depending upon the time of day.

Bales of alfalfa with Mount Diablo in the distance

On the other side of the oleander are alfalfa fields. I hear some kind of machines in the distance, tractors or threshers running 24/7, through the night and day. The smell is clean and pleasant. Unless, of course, you have allergies.

Continuing on along the higher road, I arrive at the Owl Harbor office, with its wide covered patio surrounded by a low redwood railing. There are red geraniums in terra cotta pots and a large grill, an alcove with the ice machine and a notice board with the local tides and currents listed. There are lounge chairs with pretty cushions and several hanging humming bird feeders.

At Owl Harbor there are various dogs laying around, depending upon who is working. If Devery is behind the desk her grey schnauzer Max greets you. If Curtis is behind the desk then Gus the French bulldog is laying around somewhere. Gus doesn't greet anybody. He's not a greeter dog. He just waits around for Curtis. Basically, Gus goes wherever Curtis goes, even on the new green tractor.

Every morning Devery pulls her wagon down to the other end of the property, to the vegetable garden, where she collects whatever is coming ripe in the community garden that day: garlic, tomatoes, zucchini, and eggs from the chickens. Dozens of chickens, in two separate pens. One rooster in each pen, strutting around, hens falling over themselves to get out of his way. They remind me of my grade school campus in Southern California, where the nuns all lived in tiny bedroom cubicles behind the grade school while the priest lived in a big two story house with a housekeeper. He was driven around in a big black car by a driver. Huh. How the mind does wander in the Delta.

The vegetables and eggs are displayed on the counter in the Owl Harbor office like jewels at Tiffany. They are offered gratis to Marina Tenants, even recent ones like me. The tomatoes have names like "Black Prince". There is a large coffee can behind the eggs over on the corner table. A subtle notice on the can reads: Chicken Feed Donations.

Owl Harbor eggs

Owl Harbor to Bedroom One and back again
10 am – 12:32 pm, 13.2 NM round trip. Max speed 5.9 knots, averaged 2.7 knots

7.5.17 When I arrived Bedroom One was full of kids floating around on blow-up toys and stand up paddleboards, shooting each other with waterguns.

Wild Tribe of Now and Zen

Once I had lowered sail I was invited to raft up with Tony Bourque and Patch Garcia, s/v Now and Zen, a Newport 30. Patch and Tony's kids, Sarah, Edie and Jake, climbed aboard long enough to eat.

We all crowded into the cockpit and Patch gave everybody a zip lock bag full of M & Ms and gummie bears. Even me. My own private candy bag. It was one of my favorite sailing days ever. Later on, back in Owl Harbor for the night, my feet found melted green gummie bears on Dura Mater's cabin top. The day was totally worth sticky toes.

Owl Harbor to Pirate's Lair Marina 7.5 nm Max speed 6.1 knots, average = 2.1 knots.

7.6.17 The next day, after scraping the gummie bears off DM's cabin top, we sailed from Owl Harbor to Korth's Marina under mainsail only. We waited until lunch time, and by then it was very hot: 95 degrees, so I raised the beach umbrella, stuck it into the winch holder. No need for the winch because it was too hot to move around enough to unfurl the jib. The goal du jour was to stay under the umbrella.

Dura Mater at Pirates Lair

We sailed all the way in and up to the guest dock, which has just enough room for two shallowish-draft boats. I walked up to the restaurant, ordered a tuna melt and chatted with the waitress while eating it at the counter. In the air conditioned restaurant. Yeah. That felt good.

Owl Harbor to the Mokelumne River Bridge
8:28– 10:40 am. 6.46 nm average 3.2 knots

7.17.17 Monday morning DM and I sailed from Owl Harbor to the B&W Resort. We left in the gentlest of breeze and turned left just past River's Edge Marina, sailing through the little slough in between the levee road and San Joaquin River. We drifted past the Spindrift Marina, with its motor yachts tucked away in their covered slips, boats from places like Petaluma and Denver and Portland. Passed within ten feet of a couple sitting on their back boat porch drinking their morning coffee. They smiled and waved, just like people do everywhere. Well, maybe not in Oakland.

Except for a couple of fishing boats I didn't see anybody else. Lots of birds, though. Cranes and quacking creatures. Certainly no other sailboats. What's up with that? Where are the sailboats?

By 9 am it was already real hot, so I raised my beach umbrella. Lucky for me Pelagic was steering. DM, Pelagic and I continued on until we got to the tip of the Delta Loop, then we turned to port at Pirates' Lair Marina and headed up the Mokelumne River. Still in the flood, and then we were on a broad reach. Very slowly the wind picked up, the river widened and curved ahead of us.

We passed Moore's Riverboat Restaurant with its big deck, long dock and inviting boat slips. It might be the Sam's of the Delta. There was a small sailboat tied up on an end dock. Then we were on a close reach and DM was going 6 knots effortlessly. A few more tacks, one more curve in the river and there was the Mokelumne River Bridge in front of us.

My understanding was that bridge-tenders prefer to see your boat before they start the process of stopping traffic. I used channel 9 to call the bridge operator: "Mokelumne River

Bridge, this is the sailboat Dura Mater approaching from the south. Do you read me?" No answer. I tried again. No answer. I reached for my handheld and called again. This was my first bridge and we were still in the flood. I felt like I was flying toward it. So much for planning ahead.

Finally the bridge-tender responded.

"I see you," she said. "Do you plan to sail through or motor through?"

"Well," I responded, "I have good wind, so I'll sail through." She did ask.

Immediately I was horrified to hear the Ding! Ding! Ding! of a train approaching, except that I was the train! I watched as all the trucks and cars stopped on the roads. The swing bridge started to move sideways for my little sailboat and all of a sudden my progress toward that bridge seemed to be pitiably slow.

Have I mentioned that Dura Mater had been having battery issues? One battery worked but the other one? Not so much. I was trying so hard to eek out a little more speed with my sails that I didn't go below to switch to the #2 battery which works to start the engine. So there we were, making everybody wait. And wait. I send my apologies out to everyone who waited for us that day.

As we sailed past the bridge operator on her platform above the water, I waved and thanked her. She leaned over and yelled "Most sailboats motor through!" To which I replied, "Sorry!" But that's a lie. From now on I will always wait until I am much closer to bridges before I call. I will circle 'round until the bridge-tender decides to open and I will be sure to use my engine. But I'll never be sorry that I really did sail through my first swing bridge, up the Mokelumne River. It makes me feel guilty but happy to recall it.

B & W MARINA

Dura Mater and I have been in the Delta for more than two weeks. They are the hottest two weeks I have ever experienced. I can't stand on the sole of the cockpit without my Hanalei Bay rubber "slippers". I'm surprised they haven't melted. All my chocolate has melted. A small mirror was attached to the wood above my porta-pottie with sticky back tape. The sticky back melted and the mirror fell off and cracked. The winches are so hot to the touch that I have to wear sailing gloves just to wrap the sheets around them. It's a jungle out there.

Arriving at B& W, we parked just beyond the fuel dock, next to the fish gutting table. It was 99 degrees. I staggered into the cafe, light headed from the heat. Inside is a terrific, well stocked market. Lots of top shelf liquor, plenty of low shelf liquor, too. There were "slippers", sunhats, toiletries, engine supplies like impellers and gas additives. There were fishing lures, spools of line and lots of candy. Many choices for soft drinks and a great selection of beers. There is a pool table in the middle of the café and several small tables with red and white checked oilcloth tablecloths. What's oilcloth? It's that material that rubberized rain jackets are made from.

The B&W café serves a limited menu of microwaveable or toastable food. Interestingly, it serves espresso, cappuccino and lattes, too. Most impressive: the B&W café has a soft serve machine with chocolate, vanilla, and chocolate/vanilla swirl!

"Do you like your soft serve in a cup or a cone?" asked the pretty girl behind the counter. Instead I walked over to the ice cream fridge and got myself an orange sherbet pushup.

Yep. They have 'em. Worth the sail, if you ask me. Then, while I caught my breath I sat down on the swivel stool at the counter (there's a counter!) and ordered lunch. An English muffin with jelly. It arrived perfectly toasted, and I was again asked my preference. Strawberry or grape jelly? The jelly arrived in a big quart jar, and I was handed a spoon. That's the kind of place B&W Resort is.

Little kids love B&W and there were a lot of 'em running around outside. In a well-behaved way, don't get me wrong. No yelling. Well, not loud yelling. No loud laughing. Well, not too loud laughing. They were awful cute. If you don't like little kids, you might not like B&W Resort. If you have your own little kids, you all might like B&W Resort. Your kids sure will.

The kids' parents all have motor boats. I don't know what kind of motor boats because I'm not a motor boat person, but they were all shiny and brightly colored, like big toys. Sitting in the bow of his parents' boat as they exited past the fuel dock, one little tow-headed boy looked slowly up the length of DM's luffing sail. He turned his head and I heard him say, "Mama! Look! I've never seen a real sailboat before." Which says a lot.

What does it say to me? Why, it says that poor child may have doting parents who like to spend time with him in quiet, bucolic settings. And those parents may have expensive boats and BIG engines. But I can see into that child's future. That child faces the inevitable day when he'll realize that he has been deprived. And who knows where that may lead? Sailboat deprivation: a diagnosis with its own ICD-10 code. Look it up. Go on!

INTERVIEW WITH MARVELL AND LOREN FRENCH

During my first visit to B & W Marina I wandered down to the sandy beach there, at the confluence of the Mokelumne and San Joaquin Rivers. There are stone steps that lead right down into the water and once I was no longer able to stand the water began to carry me downriver. It was my first time in the water of the Delta and the strength of the current caught me off guard. When I came up out of the water I noticed a large group of people sitting around together in a big circle. They looked happy and we smiled at each other as I approached.

I introduced myself and we chatted for a few minutes. When I asked if I could interview them they simply nodded, stood up, wrapped beach towels around their waists and followed me to a picnic table. Marvell knew exactly what I wanted. The first thing she said was: "Boaters tell stories. They all have different ones."

Turns out Marvell and Loren French have been coming to the B&W for more than 50 years together. The group included their children and grandchildren, so that makes Mr. and Mrs. French the patriarch and matriarch respectively.

The grandchildren were milling around, beautiful, healthy and respectful.

The joke in the family is this: As the grandchildren begin considering their future husbands and wives, the first quality they begin to look for in a potential spouse is whether or not he or she likes "boating". Because if their beaus don't like boats, or they don't like B & W? They're out of the running.

Loren started coming to B & G Marina when he was nine years old with his parents. Loren is 71 and Marvell is 69. He is proud of Marvelll, who speaks five languages. She still works full time at a bank in Fresno. She is Norwegian, came here as a child and met Loren when she was 15. They married when she was 18 and he was 20. They will celebrate 50 years of marriage in August of this year.

Mr and Mrs French both talked at the same time. The only reason I quote Marvell more often is because she sat closest to the microphone. It was a remarkable experience. I smiled at them both, trying to smile equally, hoping that I would be able to discern some coherence from the audiotape afterwards.

Sitting at a picnic table in the shade with wet towels wrapped around our waists, my new friends Mr. and Mrs. French and I chatted for more than an hour. Here's what they had to say:

Loren: *We got married in '67. I'm a fortunate man. I grew up boating.*

Marvell: *My father was a fisherman in Norway and ... I always loved the water. Then, when we met [indicates Loren] and I found out that [his family] were boating, that's how we ended up coming up together to the Delta. He'd been coming here since he was nine and then when we got married I was 18 and he was 20, we came here for a couple of weeks with his family on the Delta and ... I loved it. Loved it. 1000 miles of waterways, you can do all kinds of things.*

We've been coming up here ever since. Every year the family vacation comes to B & W. B & W was owned by Botts & Wilson, which were the two couples that owned it when [Loren and his family] came up here. When he came up here, we came up here. Then the Deek family bought it some time in the 70's and so Loren's parents were still alive. They knew that family, too. We would all come up here.

Loren: *We've been coming up here longer than the [current] owners.*

Marvell: *We have some of the history, some of the pictures and the movies that his parents used to take. We've never missed a year. Well, we missed B & W a couple of years in the flood but we were over at Bethel Island, so we just went to a different marina for two years. Then we [came] back here because it's kind of the best place on the Delta.*

The nice thing about B & W is that it is still a family oriented place. Sometimes you get the people that are coming in for the weekend who are a little bit rowdy. But mostly it's a family-oriented place. It's a great place to bring your kids. I think it's a great place for adults to have their vacation, too, because you're not having to deal with the kids all the time because they're off playing or boating.

Most of the time when our kids were growing up we would take our ski boats and the other families that came with us and across the San Joaquin up this way there were beaches. You could actually set up on the beaches and you'd take your picnic and do all that stuff for the day.

Jackie: What do you remember from the very first time you came to the Delta?

M: *The first time we came up here it was amazing to me because there was so much water. We could go so many places. You could boat up to Sacramento, you could boat up to the Bay, you could boat down to Stockton. Whatever. I just loved being in the water over anything.*

In 1968 we bought this little Glaspar G3 and we bought it for $700. We called it Master Charge because we got our very first credit card to establish credit. [Loren is laughing] That's what we put it on.

That summer we had our own boat and then we got into our own cabin so we had our cabin and his folks had theirs. All of us came up all these years together. We didn't have children for seven years, so when our two daughters over there [gestures toward them sitting in lawn chairs on the lawn] *were born, we were waterskiing and fishing.*

I would do the fishing with the men. Because of my Scandinavian background, I love fishing. I'd catch more fish than they would because my dad was a great fisherman and he would take me out. I'd catch a fish and then when I'd pull it up, [the other fishermen] would put their pole in where ever I was.

Jackie: What's your secret?

M: *To be patient. They were always reeling it in and checking their bait. You don't need to check your bait. I always knew to be quiet and still and patient with it. My father wasn't a fisherman by trade, he was just a very good fisherman because that's what all the Norwegians do.*

My father was a master plumber. He had a smaller boat. A 30' double ender. We'd go out in that. When we came to America we didn't really do any of that boating stuff until I met Loren. I was fifteen and his family boated and so we started boating together. Even our little Glaspar G3 which was all of 16' long, we would trailer it down to Long Beach and go out in the ocean.

L: *We would be out the breakwater and clear over to Catalina.*

M: *We would boat all around. One time we were coming back and there were these swells. The Coast Guard were out there. We were always the only people out there. We were safe. We went boating every weekend, if not every other weekend on Saturdays. We went out of Long Beach. Then in the summers we would come up here. We would trailer the boat up here.*

All these years we would come. So our kids have been coming, too. One of them is 43, the other one is 39. They've both been married for twenty years so now their kids, our six grandkids, come every year. We all have a family vacation. Fourth generation. [Marvell leans over and talks to a child who has wandered over: "We're interviewing, babe."] *That's Noah, he's our youngest grandson.*

L: *The girls are pretty good looking girls, my grandkids, and they're previewing boyfriends. One of the primary pre requisites are: "Do you like boating? Would you like to go to the Delta?"*

M: *You have to like the Delta. In fact Madeline, the [granddaughter] who is nineteen, had a boyfriend and he didn't like it up here. So that was the end of that. His family had never boated and I think he just didn't enjoy it.*

L: *That ended. [laughs] You're gone! He was reluctant to get involved. He wanted to just sit and watch things going on. You can't do that if you boat.*

M: *You've always gotta be wakeboarding or waterskiing, which we did for years and our kids learned it all and they did it for years and now we watch the grandkids. When Loren's mother passed away, which was in 1998, she left Loren this envelope. They had a strong box where all the will and everything, and I knew where everything was because she wanted me to take care of stuff.*

He opens up this envelope, and it was the deed to their cabin property which was down just south of Bakersfield. She had said, "Some day this will become your yacht."

We said [to each other] "We have to spend this money on what she wanted us to spend it on. So we sold the cabin property and then we bought our second boat. That's what we did. We could have actually not gone as big but we liked this one, it took us like five years to find it, we just started seventeen years with it. We love it. Our boat is fiberglass on the outside, the hull is, but all the wood is teak.

L: *It's actually an Albin, but there were only two made. Same brand as the Albin Vega, same company. They had these made in Taiwan. Albin was Swedish. In Sweden they made motors and then when they came over they made sailboats.*

J: Is it called Master Charge, too?

M: *No, it's called Second Chapter, which kind of fits into the second chapter of your life. The kids are gone, and yeah, the grandkids were just starting and that kind of thing. The fortunate thing was that that was the name of the boat, we didn't have to change anything. It just kinda fit perfect.*

J: What kind of changes have you seen in the Delta?

M: *There's not as many beaches, not as much sand.*

L: *All of these levees that you see were thick with trees. You've read Hal Schell, you can see all the trees. That's how the whole thing was. Pittsburgh on up was heavy with trees. One year we came up, we went, "Where the heck did the trees go?" During the winter the Army Corp of Engineers spent the winter cutting them all down.*

J: What year was that?

L: *It was wonderful. [Sighs] It was before we got married. It'd be the early 60s. They felt like the trees were impinging on the levees, the root system. I guess logically there's something there. They wanted to actually put in the rip rap blocks but they didn't want to mess with trees. Typical Army Corps of Engineers overthinking everything.*

M: *We've probably covered every inch of water you could go on. There are so many little towns and restaurants along the way, like if you're in Isleton over here, the places to eat that have been around forever. Tonight we're actually driving up to Walnut Grove to Locke. There's this place called Al the Wop's. We're having dinner there tonight. Everybody has the places they like to go.*

L: *This is the Delta Loop, where we're sitting. It goes all the way around and comes back to highway 12. It's covered with marinas and restaurants. The restaurants come and go, people go to them, then they go out, then somebody else buys them.*

Mr. French tells me that in the 55 years he's been coming here, Dura Mater is only the second sailboat that he has seen at B & W Marina. I thank them both profusely for the interview and then I go for another swim. I watch their grandchildren splashing in the water, their parents vigilant nearby.

Then I make my way back to the B & W office where I pay $20 to remain tied up at the guest dock closest to the marina entrance. At 7:56 pm it is just starting to cool off and I am too tired to sail back to Owl Harbor. This heat has eviscerated me. The showers are underneath the office/snack bar/store. They are simple but very clean. There is plenty of hot water and the water pressure is strong.

I will have to pay close attention to the depth tomorrow morning because the water is very thin here. Dura Mater is the lone sailboat in a crowd of stylish ski-boats, all painted Ferrari colors. We are sitting in the mud anyway. It would have been hard to leave.

B&W Marina to Pirates Lair 6:28 – 8 am

7.1817 Tuesday morning I wake up at 5:45 am to the sound of traffic on Highway 12 crossing the nearby Mokelumne Bridge. Run along the levee road, which has "No Trespassing" signs. Didn't get arrested. By the time I raise my sails to leave at 6:28 am it is low tide, which my Humminbird depth finder reads as 5.5'. DM has a 4.5' draft, so that seems do-able. Drift out of the marina with my hummingbird chirping, telling me that DM is sliding through some mud. A minor inconvenience and my keel is probably cleaner because of it. It is not the first time, just the first time this day.

I hail the Bridgetender on VHF channel 9: "Mokelumne River Bridge, Mokelumne River Bridge, Mokelumne River Bridge, this is the sailboat Dura Mater approaching from the north." This is quite a mouthful early in the morning before coffee, but I manage it. This time I turn on my engine and zoom through. No truck drivers will be driven crazy today.

We arrive at Pirates Lair Café at 8 am, a perfect time for scrambled eggs, English muffin and coffee. Leaving Korth's we start to sail back to Owl Harbor by drifter.

Loren and Marvell French

As we mosey along just outside Korth's Marina Mr. and Mrs. French come up behind us in a long, low speed boat. I look back and see them laughing. They ask if Dura Mater and I are stuck. I lie and assure them that Dura Mater and I are fine, thank you. Sailboats just go slow, dontcha know? They keep laughing, rev their powerful outboard engine and zoom away, waving. They knew we were in the mud.

7.29.17 Following a visit to Oakland for a week of business, I arrive back in Owl Harbor to find that both Dura Mater's batteries are dead. I am not in the habit of using shore power, but I plug into it now. I will see if the batteries are charged by tomorrow morning. What drained them? I have no idea. DM's lights are all LED except the steaming and deck lights, and I didn't leave them on when I left her last time.

Well, I suppose I did leave my chart plotter plugged in. And my laptop. And maybe my little Bluetooth speaker, too. Uh oh. This battery business is a new puzzle for me to work through.

After a chat with Curtis I decide to drive into Rio Vista, where I shop for groceries at Lira's. When I return I notice that DM's rigging is full of spider webs and the chocolate is all melted. Aside from that and the batteries, Dura Mater seems just fine, though. While I consider my options I prepare an early dinner. Rotisserie chicken, sliced tomato, Havarti cheese and risotto, cooked on my one burner butane stove. I have walnuts from my mother's farm. Coffee is already in the French press, ready to go in the morning. I brought my running shoes with all the best intentions to use them tomorrow morning, when it is cooler than now.

THE VOICE OF REASON

8.2.17 There are phenomena in the Delta known as The Voices of Reason. They occur when people visit from Outside Over There. Since only three guests have visited Dura Mater and me in the Delta I have very limited data so far, and this is my first trip so let's wait to see if additional experience confirms the need for further study.

The Voice of Reason came to collect me a few days after I arrived in Owl Harbor. He came in the middle of the day, when it was already wicked hot. I encouraged him to arrive early, when it is cool and lovely, but The Voice of Reason thinks like a city person, so he waited a bit to avoid the traffic.

Well, of course no one drives from Oakland to the Delta in the middle of the week. Anybody can see that from the traffic on the other side of the freeway. But there is no arguing with The Voice of Reason, so I trudged up to the levee road in the blazing heat when he arrived at 10:30 am.

He rolled down the window of the air conditioned car and blinked. "It's hot!" Yes it was hot. It's hot every day here, but the Really Hot would arrive later. He rolled the window back up and smiled at me through the glass.

"Lunch?" I mouthed?

"Sure. Get in." He replied.

"Let's sail. It's cool on the water. There's a breeze out there. It will only take ½ hour."

"But we have a car," said the Voice of Reason.

"But we have a boat," I insisted. "I don't know why we should drive a car when we have a perfectly good sailboat."

"Because it's air conditioned in here." The Voice of Reason waited me out. I could feel the heat melting my rubber flip flops, so I sighed and got in. We drove to Korth's Marina, had a nice lunch at the diner there, then drove back to J Dock.

"Come have a cup of coffee on the boat before we go back. The cockpit is shaded," I lied.

We walked down the dock to Dura Mater. I got my beach umbrella out and stuck it in the winch holder. When we sat real close there was shade for both of us, and there was a nice little breeze. There is almost always a nice breeze in the Delta, something Voices of Reason tend to overlook.

He pointed to a boat further down the dock. The s/v Stink Eye sported a perfectly situated triangular tarp:

> "Why don't you have one of those?"
>
> Then he eyed a ski boat motoring by us. It had a bright red bimini that matched its shiny gelcoat.
>
> "Or one of those?"

The bimini provided shade to everybody sitting on its white leather seats and all their margarita glasses, too.

I told him about my conversation with the nice man at Pirates Lair diner a week earlier. The man told me that he had just paid $1000 for a bimini for his small motor boat. "It was worth every penny," he told me proudly. And I believe him. However, a bimini is not worth $1000 to me because I already have a beach umbrella.

After we drank our coffee it was time to go back to Oakland.

"Well, this is a nice place here," The Voice of Reason conceded. "Maybe next time we'll sail."

Mebee. Mebee not. But hope springs eternal.

8.9.17 A week later as I returned to Owl Harbor from Oakland in my car I passed a herd of sheep. Cattle and goats I've seen, but this was my first sight of sheep. I pulled over to the side of the narrow gravel road and walked closer to see them up close. They walked up to the electric fence to see me up close. They drink from a large cistern at the road's edge, near to the road so it can be refilled from a truck. No matter how nicely I called, they were only briefly interested in me.

Sheep on Twitchell Island

They came for the water, not the human. My conclusion is that sheep are not at all like dogs.

I arrived back at Owl Harbor to find Curtis and two of the local kids picking black figs from a tree just the other side of the levee road across from Dura Mater. The tree grew from a cutting given to Curtis by a former tenant of Owl Harbor, a Sicilian who gives cuttings of the tree to people as wedding gifts. Three years ago the cutting he gave Curtis was two feet tall – Curtis gauged the height with his hands. Today it towered above us, laden with green and ripening black figs. From the Island of Malta, Curtis told me, called Black Malta figs. Delicious. We picked them from the limbs and popped them into our mouths.

While we talked a big racket starts up on the other side of the levee, and I walk up like a Curious George to see what is going on. Javier is riding the most elaborate contraption. It looks like a rototiller and he steers it back and forth on the water of the slough. Javier and his family live at Owl Harbor, and he has worked with Devery to recreate the Marina.

Curtis told me the machine used by Javier is called an "aquatic weed thresher" and that Seven Mile Slough has been cleared of much of the water hyacinth that was beginning to encroach upon the docks. It seems to be an ingenious machine: Like a floating John Deere tractor. I asked if I could drive it but Curtis said "No". I asked if I could just steer and assured him that I would wear a pfd. He still said "No." I've decided that he just needs to get to know me better before he says "Yes".

Javier Lopez on aquatic weed thresher

I have called a local electrician to replace my batteries, which I've had for five years. I think I depleted my #1 by charging all my electronics overnight. It will not work to start the engine. I have another, my #2, which causes the engine to start up just fine, but it is always a good idea to have a backup, right?

THE ELUSIVE HIDDEN HARBOR

8.19.17 I had a chat with Curtis, who grew up on his family's marina, called Hidden Harbor, which he described as a sailboat harbor. His grandparents bought it years ago and his father and uncle run it still. It is on Ryer Island.

Where is this so-called Hidden Harbor? How hidden is it? I was on it. How did I get to Hidden Harbor from Owl Harbor by car? I have no idea. It was very confusing and had something to do with Highway 160 and then Highway 12.

I crossed a bridge then turned right onto a road which ended at a ferry called the "Real McCoy II Ferry". I got on the ferry, which is free, but then on the other side I pulled over to the side of the road, confused. A man wearing a cowboy hat slowed down in his pickup truck and told me to turn around and get right back on the ferry again, I was going the wrong way. So that's how you get there.

The Real McCoy II Ferry

Hidden Harbor is a private marina. It may or may not be on Ryer Island and the ferry might or might not be running. Seriously. Every twenty minutes it comes and cars get on and off. If the ferry isn't running then cars don't get on and off at all.

Sure enough, there was Hidden Harbor, with a big sign: PRIVATE KEEP OUT. Huh. So I pulled over and parked. I walked past the PRIVATE KEEP OUT sign and past the NO TRESSPASSING sign and over to the office, which didn't seem much used. Handwritten notes tacked to the wall next to the door listed two different men's names: Jeff and Scott, with a phone number for each of them. Eeny meeny minee: Scott. I used my cell phone.

"Hello?"

"Hi, my name is Jackie Philpott and I have a sailboat."

"What kind?" Now this was a sailor's question.

"A Cal 2-27. Can I talk with you about your marina? I'm at your office."

"Sure. Be right there." I hung up and watched Scott as he emerged from the Marina's shop. We shook hands and I explained that I was interested in his marina. I mentioned that people had told me he was not easy to reach. He nodded, wiping his hands on a rag. He'd been working on something mechanical. I mentioned that someone had told me that when people left a phone message on his machine no one called them back. He said, "Yeah, there's a reason for that." That's all he said. No more explanation was forthcoming.

Scott's parents bought Hidden Harbor 35 years ago when he and his brother were in their early twenties. Scott said what they bought was essentially "two holes in the mud".

Entrance to Hidden Harbor Marina

Together the family developed the marina with its docks and outbuildings and at least three beautiful homes facing Steamboat Slough. I admired the established trumpet vines that curled up and along the tall redwood fences that surround the houses and walked the well maintained gravel roads that circle around the two parts of the marina.

There are separate entrances to Hidden Harbor, lined by mimosa trees and huge oleander bushes. Scott explained that entrances to the marinas are blocked at waterline to keep out the encroaching water hyacinths, and sailors are asked to call ahead to enter. The day I visited there was very little evidence of water hyacinths in the marina itself, so it seems to be an effective strategy.

The marina is serene. Scott and I stood together and watched as several people raised the sail on a small boat and made its way out into the slough. The Sacramento River lay around the corner. Scott told me that the owner of the boat had bought it without knowing how to sail, but that he was learning fast. I got the impression that the owner is an older man. Scott watched them carefully, as if to make sure they didn't need assistance, then turned back to me. He explained that the sailor took his grandkids out on the newly acquired boat and they were all "learning together".

I told him that my own boat was in Owl Harbor and he indicated what looked like a small cottage. Scott explained that he had “reclaimed” a barge boat that had previously been derelict at Owl Harbor. He had added a cupola and there it rested at the river’s edge, a home for someone.

When Hidden Harbor has slips available, there is a month long lease requirement. What are the amenities at Hidden Harbor? Well, there are showers and bathrooms. It's real pretty and on the day I visited it was sun drenched and utterly quiet. If you want to be left alone in a quiet marina close to Rio Vista, Hidden Harbor is a very good choice. The docks are not new. There is no community room or yacht club. The slip rates are probably reasonable, although I didn't ask. I’ve said this before: There are mysteries in the Delta.

8.20.17 The next day is Monday. After filling the tank with diesel and walking down to visit the chickens one last time I lay around all day reading a book and eating the last of the chocolate. In the evening I realize that, holy cow, this wind is howling!

I consult the weather app on my phone. Apparently it's 17 knots out there! My boat is getting blasted sideways on J Dock, and we're in the lee of a houseboat! According to NOAA *winds are forecast to remain generally light for both Monday and Tuesday*. Well, I hope so, because tomorrow morning is Tuesday and it will be time to leave Owl Harbor and head back to the San Francisco Bay.

I make preparations. I attach the lifesling to DM's stern rail and the 50' throw rope. Why do singlehanders have lifeslings on their boats? I have no idea. Who will throw it to me if I fall overboard? It's another one of life's mysteries, but I do it.

I've solicited two different suggestions regarding the return to the Bay Area from the Delta. A woman from down the dock recommends that if we ride the ebb all the way through Suisun Bay we'll get home faster. Jonathan Gutoff says the chop created by the ebb would make for a miserable ride, and he himself has always returned during a flood.

Owl Harbor to Benicia Marina
7:25 am - 12:36 = 5 hours motorsailed. 41 nm.

8.21.17 As I motor slowly out of Seven Mile Slough I see the great blue heron sitting in the reeds just before the Dredger. On the porch of one of the houseboats I hear chimes of the same type and timbre that I gave my daughter, Claire, for her 17 year birthday.

By 8:12 am, as we pass Bradford Island, the wind is so high the boat is already heeling. I consider the advantage of a dodger, which would be highly appreciated about now. We are in a powerful ebb. I've decided that Jonathan was right after all, but the decision has been made. It is overcast, the wind is in the mid- 20s and gusts are higher as we motor-sail past Pittsburg.

Sodden sailor

Today the area known as Middle Ground seems a completely different place than when Dura Mater and I sailed through under spinnaker at the beginning of July. It is a remarkable change.

By 9:50 am the boat is going 7.3 knots in the ebb and the Pelagic is working flawlessly, as is the Engine By Dave. The big steep waves are insistent, washing over Dura Mater's bow and me in my foul weather gear and ski goggles. I am totally soaked but luckily I brought ski goggles with yellow lenses. They are a lifesaver on this overcast, violently wet day.

The trip from Owl Harbor to Benicia seems very long and I am exhausted by the time we arrive in Benicia Marina. Our maximum speed was 8.8 knots in the ebb. As we arrive in Benicia I am so grateful to be warm again and able to change into dry clothes!

After checking in with the harbormaster I trudge up to a cafe in town and order a mushroom and spinach omelette to go. Returning to DM I set the omelette on my little fold-down table and then crawl into the v berth and sleep for five hours.

I wake and eat dinner as the sun sets, then it's back into the v berth for the rest of the night. Who knows what the rest of this trip has in store for me?

Benicia to Berkeley Marina 6:15 am – 9:30 aam. 25.1 nm
maximum speed = 11.3 knots

8.22.17 Up at 5 am, I drink strong coffee and eat a bowl of granola by Coleman lantern. At 5:55 am a ferry arrives, all shiny aluminum, with a blinding light straight into my cabin as I put on my life jacket. After dropping the key into the mail slot at the harbormaster's office Dura Mater and I leave Benicia marina at 6:15 am. There is no fooling around, thinking we might sail home part of the way today. I raise DM's mainsail because I am ever hopeful, but end up running the engine full throttle all the way back to Berkeley Marina.

By 6:47 am we are passing the entrance to Mare Island Strait @ 9.9 knots of speed with the ebb. By 8:10 am we pass the Brothers at 8.6 knots, then we enter Berkeley Marina at 9:30 am. The return from Benicia Marina to Berkeley took just 3.25 hours. The Ebb is everything. Everything is the Ebb. Was it worth the pain and suffering? Let's call it an adventure and consider it in tomorrow's new light.

INTERVIEW WITH TOM PATTERSON

11.30.17 After my first visit to the Delta I called up Tom Patterson. I've known Tom through the Singlehanded Sailing Society for years now. When I arrived at his home in El Cerrito he had pastries and strong coffee waiting for me. Then he dug around for brown sugar and real cream. Sometimes interviews are delicious.

On the dining room table he had laid out more than four full-sized charts, several books about the Delta, and photo books of his family members and friends on sailboats. To say that Tom knows a whole lot about sailing is like saying that the Pope is Catholic. Having been raised Catholic, I'm pretty sure that bit about the Pope is true. I know it's true about Tom. We talked about sailing in the Delta all afternoon. Only two hours' worth made it onto audiotape, and here's part of what he said:

The first time I went to the Delta I had no idea where I was going. I went with the Boy Scouts and I was probably about 14 years old. I'm not quite sure how we got there because, as you've seen, the Delta is an incredible maze. We went in an Owens powerboat, it was probably 26' long. Absolute classic. There was an Owens dealer in Stockton. As Boy Scouts we slept back up on the shore and the dads slept in the boat.

I now know where we went: Where we went to was the Meadows. This would have been about 1960. It was commonly called The Meadows by the people who went there but it wasn't even official. It wasn't until about 1971 that the name The Meadows even shows up on a chart. I dug out some old charts that I have and [on] one of them, I hand wrote: The Meadows.

In the 50s and 60's they used to go en masse (opens chart) up in here. This is the north fork of the Mokelumne River. The way people used to do this is they did not take their sailboats to marinas. I never ever took a sailboat to a marina in all the years of going up there.

You went up there to be away from marinas. To be out in nature. To go find a place to go to be away from other people and boats and spend time. The only other people you'd see were your friends who you might invite to come and spend time with you.

I was told, years ago, that the YRA (Yacht Racing Association) didn't schedule any races in July so people could take their boats to the Delta. That was the tradition for years. And the boats that people took to the Delta back then were the same boats that people raced in the Bay. In fact, if you look in the older books you'll see pictures of Bird boats in there.

One of my high school friends, her nickname is Steamboat. Her nickname is Steamboat because she was conceived on Steamboat Slough ... on her parents' Bird boat. Her real name is Maureen. Chrissy, my ex-wife, talked about having gone up to the Delta and sleeping with the spinnaker pole up on the bow of the boat somewhere. So this is what people did. They took their boats up there.

Now you think about that: Most of those boats didn't have an engine or if they did, maybe they had an outboard that they could push it along with. The other thing people did back then, much more than now, or maybe different from now, is that they would take their boat up someplace, they would park it for a couple of weeks. Not in a marina! No way would they go to a marina.

They'd go tie off to some trees, put on a couple of anchors, they'd have a dinghy and the boat would stay there, in that spot, for a couple of weeks. And they would dinghy ashore. They would bring a car up there, they'd have their car. If the husband or somebody needed to get back to the city they could do that. This was typical of leaving the boats up there for awhile. Certainly in the fifties and sixties.

I was re-introduced to [the Delta] in about 1976 by very good friends of mine who had been taking their boats up to the Delta for years, and went up to The Meadows. They told me they got turned on to this space from old time people at Richmond Yacht Club. They introduced me to it and that's how I ended up going there a lot. This is what people used to do. And talk about "You can't get there from here": it is an amazing place.

How you get to the north fork of the Mokelumne is part of the interesting puzzle. Technically, that [Tom gestures on the map with his finger] *is the north fork of the Mokelumne, cuz the north fork goes that way. But in order to get there you go up Snodgrass Slough and back down through Dead Horse Cut. This is actually the way you come up, this is SO shallow through here and there's a little fixed bridge and then you have to go this way cuz the actual north fork comes in this way.*

This is Dead Horse Island. If you ever go through Dead Horse Cut stay to the west side. It's usually deeper on this side. And I can't tell you what the draught is through there cuz I haven't done it now in a few years.

[Despite all the finger pointing, I was completely lost in the Delta already, but I nodded].

Now, the way I did this with my seven foot draft? High tide. If I had to do it at three o'clock in the morning, I did it at three o'clock in the morning. High tide. I spent a lot of time knowing what the tides were going to do in that area in order to be able to do it. This is actually very wide in here, you can anchor anywhere in here for a short time. One of the things that I've gotta say, about the charts: Don't believe the depths on the chart. The only thing that has been surveyed are the channels. None of the rest of this stuff has been surveyed.

Kimberly Patterson aboard Seraffyn, 1986

The first time I sailed SERAFFYN home through Middle Ground it was quite challenging. There was a big ebb and a westerly breeze causing short period, very steep wind waves. Tacking was the challenge. Frequently as I came into the wind, the boat would just stop and slide backwards. Several times I resorted to wearing around, which wasn't so bad with the added push to weather of the ebb.

Given the conditions, I really wanted to extend each tack and sailed way too close to the Naval Weapons Depot. There were no ships there so I thought I was OK until a guard in a car showed up. He waved, I waved back then tacked. On my next tack back toward the wharf, there would be the guard, waving. On about the third time he leveled his gun at me and I got the message.

I'd heard about the "sailing route" through Suisun Bay, but never tried it. It had been the route that was most commonly used to sail home back in the day when most boats were more reliant on sail than motors. You can appreciate the challenge of keeping a small outboard motor prop in the water through Middle Ground, Suisun Bay. Think Bird and Bear boats.

The answer is that they didn't motor, they sailed. If you look at the chart, north of Ryer Island is SUISUN CUTOFF. It's pretty much one long port tack from between Simmons Point and Stake Point (in the Sacramento River) through SUISUN CUTOFF most of the way to the Reserve Fleet. The tradeoff is a longer distance, but [with] much more protection from the long fetch waves of Suisun Bay.

I can say, I highly recommend that route. There have been days when I've powered through Middle Ground with little or no wind, but if there's that nasty combination of wind over ebb, try Suisun Cutoff.

INTERVIEW WITH ROB TRYON

12.17.17 In December of 2017 I learned from a friend that Rob Tryon was in town. He was staying aboard his boat LaDonna Jean in Brisbane Marina. Rob and his wife, LaDonna Buback, spent a lot of time sailing in the Delta. Besides, Rob is a great story teller and very funny. So I called ahead and sailed down to interview him.

We considered driving to a restaurant. Rob had a car in the parking lot, but I had uncooked noodles and pasta sauce on Dura Mater. Not really enough for two, and no cheese, but we cooked it up aboard LaDonna Jean. Singlehanders eat what they got. We boiled the pasta, heated up the sauce. We ate as we started the interview, so sometimes the audiotaped interview sounds like we had our mouths full of food. Which we did.

Rob: (talking with his mouth full) *I wish I had a little hard cheese but I don't.*

[Rob giggled a lot during this interview]. I could tell that it would be difficult to keep him focused. As it was, we talked for three hours.

Jackie: How did you happen to go up to the Delta?

Rob: *Ladonna and I grew up on the Columbia River. I'm from the Columbia River up near Portland, so River Delta is where I come from. They called us River Rats. There is that person in the Delta. So we clicked. Right? We just knew these people.*

LaDonna and my plans always revolve around a river because we want to go to places and sail up rivers. We were living on our boat in Newport, Oregon and this goofball named Gerry sailed in on a Cal 31. He was a retired CHP, California Highway Patrol. [laughs] Just a cantankerous old fuck. He'd get a job wherever he went as a meter maid, so he got a job there in Newport as a meter maid.

He was from one of those little towns up in the Delta. He showed me the Hal Schell book and then he had this old chart pack. It was obviously done by a yacht club up there, it was little chartlets of the little places, you know? The fingers and the five fingers in Mildred's Slough and all these little leads, you know?

I was fascinated and told LaDonna, "We should go. We should stop in San Francisco. Why don't we just spend the winter in San Francisco Bay and we'll explore the California Delta." And she said, "Wow, that sounds great."

Cruising World had started a website and they had this bulletin board called the Cruising World Bulletin Board. Ladonna mentioned on this Cruising World Bulletin Board that we were going to go to the California Delta on our way to Mexico. This was early internet. Herb McCormick [editor of Cruising World] sent her a private message [that] said, "I had a feature planned on the California Delta and the guy who was going to do it bailed on me. Do you think you can do it?" So we had a mission to do that, and that's what we did. This was 2002.

First we anchored off the mothball fleet, that was the first place we stopped in the Delta. We were on our way to Antioch but it was getting dark and we didn't want to go in. We made it through the Carquinez Bridge and then the Martinez Bridge. Then we went to Antioch. We stayed there for the winter.

We had driven down a few months before we sailed down and we looked at some different marinas. We were just looking at price. The place we were going to go was this place called Owl Harbor Marina and it was dirt cheap: Like $2.50/foot. We got there and there were meth labs. You could smell it. It was horrible. It was scary. Antioch was the next cheapest place. I'm sure that was it. It was central and it was the next cheapest place. So we brought the boat in there.

We did a bunch of boat work and we did at least three month long trips. The first one was over Thanksgiving. We wanted to see the Meadows. Everybody had said: "Oh, you gotta go to the Meadows. The Meadows is the special place." Hal Schell talks about how the Meadows is just great. So here we are, we're in our ocean boat, 5 ½' draft, middle of winter, a few days before Thanksgiving, and we're going to go to the Meadows. Because it's the middle of winter you have to make appointments for the bridges. The bridges aren't manned: it's that time of year.

So there's this bridge, it's called the Snodgrass Slough Swing Bridge, and you have to go through to get up to the Meadows. You go up to the San Joaquin, turn left at the Mokelumne River, you go all the way up the north fork of the Mokelumne River until you get to the Bridge at Snodgrass Slough and we anchored there right in front of the bridge.

Our appointment for the next day was at noon and at noon we had eaten breakfast and cleaned up and we were standing at the bridge, waiting for something to happen! This guy drives up in this pickup and he stops in the middle of the bridge and he goes,

"Am I opening for you guys?"
I go, "Yeah".
And he goes, "Oh. Okay."

He hooked his truck up to the bridge and he got in his truck and he revved the engine - it's a power take off on the truck - and it moved the bridge. And we motored in. We were in front of the bridge and we're motoring through and we slowed down and we're chatting with the guy and he asks,

"Where are you going?"
"We're going to the Meadows."
"You might not make it up there. What do you draw?"
"Just under six feet."
"Might make it up there."
"Hmm. Okay. Don't sailboats go up there all the time?"

[Rob makes a face, opens his eyes wide and shakes his head]

> *"So when you coming out?"*
> *"I don't know. A coupla weeks."*
> *He goes, "Well, I'll see ya when ya do."*

> *CUZ HE'S THE DUDE THAT OPENS THE BRIDGE!*

So we go up there. We get past the little resort area and the river sorta widens out and there's no channel markers or anything. We start running aground. BANG! BANG! BANG! It's sandy mud. So LaDonna gets in the skiff with a lead line, and she's in front of the boat sounding the channel. It took us several hours. In fact, she went up into the Meadows in the dinghy and came back and goes, "Yeah, it's just beautiful, it's right around the corner."

We just couldn't get there. We kept running aground. It's getting dark and there's a great big moon coming up. Let's just anchor right here! We'll tie the stern to a tree. Great big moon coming up, so the tide was rising. Big. Tall. Tide.

We had spent an evening with Hal Schell. He gave us some very strict instructions. He told me two things. He told me lots of things: the guy could talk like crazy. Two things stick with me:

> *One: stop moving at mid tide. Only move on a rising tide. If you're exploring – gunkholing, which was what we wanted to do. We wanted to get off the beaten path and find our own little nooks and crannies.*

The other piece of advice that has stuck with me: If you see birds standing, don't go there. Perfect, right?

[Rob and I laugh and laugh]

So the tide's coming up, it's past mid tide, we're having trouble getting through here and we just decided to call it.

Mid tide is where the tide is half up or half down. If you're going, as long as it's still flooding, you're fine. But once you're past the half way point? Quit moving, because if you run aground then you might be there for awhile. Especially because we'd had this big, full moon and we didn't want to run aground at a big high tide cuz then we knew we'd be there for awhile.

We quit as that moon started coming up and we put a bow anchor out and I tied the stern to a tree using the skiff. This is our first big cruise. It was Thanksgiving. We had gotten down in October and this was Thanksgiving.

Snodgrass Slough. Going to the Meadows. That's the only way to get there. The pictures that we saw? There were big boats, big sailboats anchored there. So, whatever. Especially with rivers, things silt in, move around....

[Rob shrugs his shoulders in a 'the world is mysterious' kind of way]

LaDonna and I, we both grew up without television, so television is kind of a thing for us. It's one of the things we do for entertainment: we look at television. We were at this garage sale in Antioch and LaDonna bought this little tv for $10. It was this little tiny, colored tv. Back then it was just broadcast tv? All the tv towers are there in the Delta, so we got great reception! There was this tv show where they put people on an island and left them there. They would shoot bows and arrows, it was just all sorts of fun.

We were watching this tv show, crowding around our little tiny $10 tv and LaDonna goes:

"Huh! I think we're run aground!"

"We didn't run aground. We're in a nice big hole here."

She goes, "No. The boat's feeling weird."

"You don't know what you're talking about."

So the tide goes out, tide goes out, tide goes out. By 4 in the morning we're all the way on the side. I'm in the V Berth lying athwarts ship with my feet on the ceiling and

LaDonna's on the settee in a lee cloth? With the cat. Every few minutes something shifts in a locker or the cabinets or a pencil fell out of here or something, and LaDonna would go:

"Fuck!"
Rob: "What's the matter?"
LD: "Shut up! I told you we were aground!"
R: "I didn't think we were!"
LD: "You never NEVER think we are!"
We're yapping at each other. It's Thanksgiving morning.
LaDonna: "Great Thanksgiving! You had to anchor us here and we're in the mud! We're probably going to die!"
Right then the bilge pump cycled.
LD: "What's that?"
R: "It's the bilge pump cycling."
LD: "I know!"
Then it cycled again. We both jumped up.
LD: "You look at the prop shaft, I'll check the thru hulls."

I jumped in the engine room and she's down there looking at the thru hulls. We only had seven thru hulls on that boat. She looked at the thru hulls real quick and I'm still in the engine room trying to sort things out, get my flashlight in the right place. LaDonna is in the bilge and she's got her flashlight shining down inside the bilge at the bilge pump.

LD: "Oh! I know what it is! It's syphoning back through.

What happened is, we were laying on our side. We didn't have a refrigerator. We used an ice box. I had this little vented loop that emptied the ice as it melted into the bilge and it would cycle the pump. When I put the bilge pump in I had put this gooseneck in up under the toe rail. We were laying on our side and it would pump out and then put it back in. So we went, "Oh! Okay!" Nobody's cranky anymore.

We finally floated off and we moved to a spot where we had at least three or four feet under us the whole time, and LaDonna made this from-scratch feast! With a whole turkey and special green beans and mashed potatoes and gravy and a pecan pie and a pumpkin pie that had this toasted crumble top.

That was our Delta Thanksgiving. It was our first Thanksgiving on the boat and we made a tradition from then on that we would do these little Thanksgiving cruises wherever we were. We ran aground a hundred times that day. We kept running aground and LaDonna would come over with the skiff and push the nose off.

J: Did you have a depth finder?

R: *Yeah. But, you know ... we had to find our way in there. We were out of a navigable channel so ... it changes. What's really interesting about that particular trip was that we never did get our big boat into the Meadows. We stayed anchored where we were for a couple of weeks and explored that whole area with the dinghy. We spent a day in the Meadows in the dinghy. What was great? We were there at the end of November, early December and there was nobody there.*

We had an Avon inflatable with a ten horsepower outboard. We took our skiff all the way to I-5 [Interstate 5]. Up Snodgrass Slough. We saw I-5 and the water was so thin we kept having to put the outboard up so it was just barely in the water. We were travelling in eight or nine inches of water.

[Dishes clatter on the audiotape. We were done eating. Rob pushed aside the dishes and cutlery.]

Rob: *We have our boat set up to live away from the dock, so everything works on the boat just like on the dock. I remember one time we were in Georgiana Slough. The top half of Georgiana Slough is the most beautiful part of the Delta. It's got these overhanging trees. There's a lot of bamboo that's growing there. It's really lush and beautiful.*

It's quiet because of all the trees and there's only a road on this one side and it's like an oil dirt track farm road so there's not a lot of traffic.

The other thing about Georgiana Slough is there's a swing bridge there, then there's a bascule bridge right on the old Sacramento just a few hundred yards up from the Georgiana Slough [bridge]. Down about three miles there's a no wake zone. We anchored there because everybody had to slow down.

It was middle of the winter, I think this was our February trip and it was getting dark about 4:30- 5 oclock. Our boat was rigged as a yawl and I would hang an anchor light on the end of our mizzen boom. The sheriff would come by every night just about when I'm hanging up my anchor light. We waved at each other. This went on four or five nights and finally he stopped.

"Are you really from Portland Oregon?"
I said, "Yeah."
"How did you get your boat here?"
"We sailed it here."
He said, "You mean in the ocean?"
"Yes, in the ocean."
"Well, how long are you gonna be here?"
I said, "Well, I don't know. For a couple of weeks. Is that okay?"
"What are you doing here?"
"Living. ExpLoreng. Kind of checking things out."
"Man," he says. "You guys picked the best winter."

The weather was just phenomenal. There was no rain and the sun was shining. We're from the Pacific Northwest where you put on thermals in September and you don't take 'em off till May. I'm pretty sure this was 2002 and it was a spectacular winter. 2002 or 2003. Just a great time.

We saw that sheriff several other times and he always would come over and say 'hi'. Nobody else ever asked us what we were doing or why we were there. I don't think there were very many people anchored out at all back then. I wonder if there's more now.

Remember I told you about that shitty marina? Owl Harbor? And that it was a crack place? LaDonna and Richard [Spindler, founder of Latitude 38] *were sitting around one day. It was the middle of the recession and nobody was doing the HaHa. The year before 70 boats had signed up for the Baja HaHa when normally they have 300 boats? People weren't travelling.*

Richard said, "We need to put on an event that has people travelling in their backyard."

LaDonna said, "Let's do something in the Delta.

"Yeah! You guys know about the Delta! What do we call it?"

So they went back and forth, and I don't know who 'did' it, but when you've got the HaHa and the TaTa ... it became the Doo Dah .... LaDonna got ahold of a bunch of people at marinas up there and said, 'We want to bring twenty five boats up". They limited entries that first year. The first year we made Stockton Sailing Club the final party.

LaDonna had gotten ahold of this guy named Peter Yates who was a South African that lived up on Bethel Island. He said, 'Hey, you stop here and I'll throw you guys a party.' So we do the Doo Dah and we meet Peter, who has a Wiley 34 named Coyote and a Grand Banks 42 named after some woman, and he had these two bridge tenders which are diesel army boats about 35' long, real low in the water, a couple of hobie cats and some jetskis. And a whole bunch of booze.

He took everybody out to this little sandbar in Frank's Tract, which used to be an island but the levee broke. And we had a party. It was just fantastic. That night we went to the Rusty Porthole restaurant, real close to where the party was, and they opened it just for us and Peter's musicians. He brought some musician friends and a bunch of instruments. I was a musician in my professional life so we played. It was a magical thing, really really a lot of fun.

This was the first Doo Dah, I don't remember [the year], 2008 or 2009, something like that. We were going to do it again, it had been a big success. This time Latitude wanted to monetize the Doo Dah, so they got some sponsors and we met Devery.

LaDonna came home and said, "Do you remember that marina that we stopped at with the meth labs? Owl Harbor? I got a call from a woman. She and her husband just bought it and they're fixing it up and they want us to come there."

I said, "Honey, either they gotta have a ton of money or really be motivated people to clean that shithole up." Right? They were not only super motivated people, but they were well funded. They had both things going for them and they took that shithole and ... have you seen it lately? It's incredible! Devery's husband Casey and his sister had bought the marina and they hired Devery to run it. We started making Owl Harbor the centerpiece of the Doo Dah because Devery would go all out. She spent $1400 to have the band. That's just what she paid for the band!

Chris and LaDonna were the dudettes. When LaDonna quit [as editor of Latitude] .... *what they did was they called it the DYI Doo Dah. If you're going to do it, do it yourself. And it was sort of a joke. We printed up some tshirts and it says: "You want a Doo Dah? Do it Yo damned self!"*

By this time the interview had gone really late into the night, so I left LaDonna Jean and walked over to climb aboard Dura Mater on the guest dock. I was unprepared for the cold, so then I went back and borrowed a tiny electric heater from Rob. But it didn't help much at all and that's how I learned that Brisbane Marina can be a really cold place in the winter.

INTERVIEW WITH CHRISTINE WEAVER

1.31.18 Before I returned to the Delta for a second summer, I decided to do some serious research. In January of 2018 I sailed over to Sam's Café in Tiburon and met with Christine Weaver. She walked down the gangplank to Sam's dock where I was tying my boat to a cleat, and we agreed to request a table in the sun. Now that's my idea of researching. Over lunch I asked her to tell me more about the Delta and also about the history of the Delta Doo Dah.

In 2009 Christine and Ladonna Bubak, former editor of the sailing magazine Latitude 38, began organizing the Delta Doo Dah, which is described as 'a summer sailing rally up river to the California Delta'. Racing editor at Latitude, Christine is widely referred to as the Delta Doodette. Here is some of our conversation:

Jackie: How did the Delta Doo Dah happen in 2009? Did you and Ladonna just sort of have an idea, as in: "Hey! Let's do this!"?

Christine: *Yeah. LaDonna and I were the co-dudettes. We were always a team. We started it together. The recession had hit and we were looking, number one, for ways to occupy our time, and number two, for things to do to support sailing and encourage people to get out and use their boats. But people didn't have money. People had more time than money. Now it's the opposite.*

We thought about doing a Delta rally that would be like the Baja HaHa, but that wouldn't cost hardly anything. So we had a low entry fee. I think the first year it might have been $49. That includes your flag and a t-shirt and a bag of goodies and free stays at the marina and some free meals. Some of the meals were comped. So that helped promote some of the Delta businesses. We had many stops.

In the middle of the week we had three free nights where people would go their separate ways. Jonathan [Gutoff] and I wanted to go to Walnut Grove and a couple of other boats went with us, but most of them went somewhere with Ladonna and Rob (Tryon). Our ultimate destination was the Stockton Sailing Club and they had a big party for us. This was in 2009. The third year was the first year that Owl Harbor signed on with us. Devery contacted us. It wasn't our idea. It was hers. They are still with us as a sponsor.

Then after Delta Doo Dah #4 there were some layoffs at Latitude and everybody who was left was overworked. The publishing industry never recovered from the recession, so even though, by 2012, things were maybe starting to look up for some other industries, the publishing industry? Everything changed radically for the publishing industry. And it never came back. So for Delta Doo Dah #5 we turned it into a do-it-yourself where we had a free sign up. If you wanted a burgee you had to pay for it. We didn't have any shirts. We still got deals from some marinas but basically you were on your own.

After Delta Doo Dah #5 LaDonna left and I decided to try to get back a little more of the event feel to it. Delta Doo Dah #10, 11 and 12 were organized rallies that were like the Baja Haha. We've always had kick off parties. They've alternated between Berkeley Yacht Club and Richmond Yacht Club. One year we had it at Tradewinds Sailing. Ann and Craig Perez have a Delta Cruising seminar so we've partnered with them and combined that with our kick-off party. We're trying different things.

J: Is this fun for you or has it become work?

C: *It's kind of both. It's a lot of work for one person to do and I would do more if I had more time but my job is pretty demanding. I also decided I didn't want the liability of leading 50 boats up the Delta where bad things can happen. Accidents. I didn't want the personal or moral liability of it. It was not a Latitude decision.*

The only money [Latitude] gets is from selling t-shirts and burgees. One year we had straw fedoras. People loved them. I didn't order enough. I didn't realize how popular they would be. If part of the idea is participation and to see as many people wearing your logo-wear as possible, you want to keep the price down. And you also don't want people to feel like it's a high end kind of thing to be part of. I want people to feel like anybody can afford it. It's the opposite of elite.

J: Okay: How about the Delta? You got me into this project. The way you wrote about the Delta in Latitude, it sounded so nice! What "hooked" *you* on the Delta?

C: *The warmth. The hot weather. The ruralness of it. The uncrowdedness of it. The fact that you could swim in the water without a wetsuit and actually spend time in the water just laying around and not feeling like if you're not swimming vigorously you're going to get hypothermic.*

The Delta Doodette

People are friendly and they'll actually talk to you. It's so different. You don't realize how guarded we are in the Bay Area. We're so overcrowded that we have to be more protective of our personal space. When you get someplace like [the Delta] that's not overcrowded, people are so much more friendly and more open. It's a much less frantic pace, for sure. Even among people who live there full time and are working. It's a whole different thing.

J: When was the very first time you went up to the Delta?

C: *The very first time I went up to the Delta on a sailboat was in 1997 in the Delta Ditch Run. I've never missed a Delta Ditch run since. I've done twenty one Delta Ditch runs.*

The Delta cruising started in 2005. I convinced Jonathan [Gutoff] of Stink Eye, a Laser 28, to do the Delta Ditch Run. He had never done it before. So he and his brother Bill and couple of other people and I did the Delta Ditch Run. We got together about a month later and one of the first things he said to me was that he wanted to try a Delta cruise after the Ditch Run the following year. So that was our first Delta cruise together. We anchored out in Frank's Tract. We did a lot of swimming and it was really hot and it was very pleasant.

J: Tell me about the spiders.

C: *Oh we get lots of spiders on our boat.*

J: So people who are deathly afraid of spiders might not like the Delta.

C: *Right.*

J: What do you do about mosquitoes?

C: *For the most part we haven't had too much trouble with mosquitoes. They do have mosquito control up there, which means they spray for them. At night we put the hatch board in and we have screens on our opening ports. I think screens are necessary. Twilight is when the mosquitoes mostly come out, so before that happens I change into long sleeves and long pants and fortunately the temperature drops at dusk as well so you're not all bundled up [when] it's 100 degrees out.*

There was one night in particular toward the end of the season. We must have been there in August. We hadn't practiced good mosquito prevention protocol so we had a cabin full of mosquitoes. I went on a rampage. I went on a mosquito killing rampage! We have an overhead light and they are kind of attracted to the light. They had already eaten their fill. They would land on the ceiling or on the walls of the cabin and I would wait for them to settle and I would smash 'em! There are still streaks of blood on the interior paint of our boat. (Christine smiles with satisfaction and takes a big bite of tortilla chip). *It was fun!*

J: What's your very favorite memory of the Delta?

C: *Probably that first year anchored in Frank's Tract ... skinny dipping in the water there. Feeling free. You don't realize how tight you are and how tense you are until that all goes away. I also recommend calling ahead if you're planning to go into a marina or a yacht club, make sure they have a spot for you.*

If you're planning to get gas or diesel, especially at a particular gas dock, call ahead. Make sure they are still open. A lot of them have closed. Some of them have had to shut down their diesel pumps. Check the hours. See if they are self-serve if you are going after hours. Just call ahead.

J: Those are great, clear suggestions. Then, what do you get when you get there?

C: *It will depend on the weather. If it's really hot, be prepared for 100 plus degrees of heat. . Make sure you have some shade on your boat . Make sure you can get in and out of the water at will. You need a swim ladder. Because you will need to get in the water. But also it can be cold. It can be chilly at night. It's almost never really hot at night so you need to bring layers to stay warm.*

J: What else would you like to say about the Delta?

C: *I would tell people not to be too nervous about it. Don't worry about running aground, don't worry about anchoring, just do it. It's a great place to learn how to do all that stuff. It's pretty forgiving.*

My other recommendation is that, unless you have a trailer boat and you're going to go back at 55 mph, allow yourself to take advantage of a weather window for your delivery back. That and to have a bailout plan in case the weather is too rough for you. That is very subjective depending on the nature of your boat. Is it a big heavy ocean going cruiser with lee cloths and a dodger? Then there probably is no bad weather.

If you have a tender little sailboat with no protection from the elements then you might want to pick a weather window and have a bail-out plan. We've bailed out at Antioch Marina where you can walk to the Amtrak and take the train back to the Bay Area or we have put into Pittsburgh and spent the night before trying again in the morning.

You can put in at Benicia Marina. You can go up to Vallejo Marina. For instance, sometimes you can get through Suisun Bay just fine but then you get into San Pablo Bay and it's like Hell! [laughs] *You turn around and go with the wind and with the waves, you get to Vallejo really quickly! Without too much fuss or muss!* [she laughs again]

If you're a yacht club member you can get reciprocals at Vallejo Yacht Club and they are very welcoming or you can go into Vallejo Municipal Marina. You have facilities there and you can walk to a restaurant if you want to, or to a store or you can take the Vallejo ferry back to the Bay Area if you really need to go to work the next day. Then come back when the weather is better and get your boat and bring it back.

So I recommend having some flexibility about your return plan and also have some flexibility in your itinerary. You might think you're only going to anchor for one night at some idyllic spot and then you find that you just don't want to leave.

Even at the end of January the outside deck at Sam's Café was unusually sundrenched yet comfortably cool. Christine and I stayed on a bit after finishing our lunches. We talked about how fortunate we are to live in the San Francisco Bay area where we are able to sail year round. Then we said goodbye to each other and went our separate ways.

SUMMER TWO 2018

DURA MATER DOES THE DELTA DITCH RUN

Most sailors in the San Francisco Bay area understand that the Delta Ditch Run is a cutthroat, competitive and crewed sailing event. It's a 67 nautical mile run from the Richmond Yacht Club, just southeast of the Richmond/San Rafael Bridge to the Stockton Sailing Club, which is, in Delta parlance: "down in the ditch".

Other people, of course, use it as a pleasurable and fun way to get to the Delta with a passel of friends and a boat full of water toys. Of course, even for those folks there is that "two boats on the water" inclination: If there are two boats on the water? It's a race!

Contrary and dim witted is the sailor who attempts The Delta Ditch Run solo and in a slow boat. And yet, that was the plan in 2018 when Dura Mater and I registered for the twenty eighth version of the race.

We were registered in the Cruising division. Boats in the cruising division are allotted four hours of motoring. Because there was no wind at the start of the race we used up those four hours before we even reached the Antioch Bridge. Way before that. Here's the whole sorry story:

On June 7, 2018 Dura Mater and I left the Richmond Yacht Club harbor to do the Ditch Run. There was almost no wind at the start and the day was very hot. I repeat. Very hot. It was so hot I thought I'd die of heat stroke. I think maybe I did die. And then I came back as a singlehander in the Delta Ditch Run.

Once under the first bridge I felt all the classic signs: first I was nauseous, then I was dizzy while taking my spinnaker down, then I started getting chills.

Uh oh. This is bad. I'm going to die out here. What was I thinking???!!! I drink a third bottle of water, take my hat off and pour another bottle over my head, then another one down my shirt. After that I set my Pelagic, look around, go down into the cabin and lay down. Aaaaaahh. Wish I could stay here out of the sun for awhile.

Under spinnaker in Carquinez Strait

Maybe I did. Next thing, I hear voices. Well, maybe only one voice. "Ahoy!"

I pop my head up out of the cabin and realize that I have drifted far over to starboard, over to where .... there was a large boat with POLICE printed in big letters on its side. The young men aboard seem a bit taken aback when they see just one person aboard, but the skipper of Dura Mater can quickly revert from surly to friendly when law enforcement is involved.

"Oh! Hi, officers!"

They look at each other. "Ah ... Ma'am, you're not allowed in this area." It seems Dura Mater and I have drifted over toward Seal Islands. Near a restricted area.

"Oh, really? Sorry! Sorry!" I turn the boat around and we immediately get stuck in the mud. I wave again, "Don't worry! I'm leaving! Don't worry! Carry on!"

I go on up to Dura Mater's bow and rock and rock, waving to the nice policemen with the big guns until we float out of the mud. We are free of the river but still in this damned race. We float on and on under that very hot sun until I hear voices. Hallucination? No. Real voices.

"Hey! It's Jackie! Hi, Jackie!" There were Synthia and Nathalie to port, not looking miserable at all. Nathalie's Figaro Envolee passed steadily by with a full crew of happy looking people. She had a huge spinnaker up, and every sunburned face was smiling. I mumbled to myself, "So that's what it's like to sail with other people aboard. Huh. Gotta try that sometime. Maybe next year. Gotta make some friends."

I decided that I should at least raise my spinnaker again, try to look like I knew what I was doing. So I did and we sailed under the Antioch Bridge and we did go slightly faster that way. Looking ahead I saw that the wind had shifted and other people were lowering their spinnakers. If racers were lowering their spinnakers you can bet I should lower mine.

We approached the point in the sailing instructions that reads, in bold print: AFTER THE ANTIOCH BRIDGE, LEAVE MARK #19 TO PORT. Of course I remembered that clearly, and we passed marker #19 to port. But then I had a bit of a struggle with the spinnaker, my ankle caught between the spaghetti and the gear shift, and before I knew it DM and I were stuck fast in the mud as the tide ebbed and the water got thinner and thinner @ 38.02274, -121.42705.

I kedged, I rocked, I used very bad language. No matter what I did, Dura Mater and I weren't going anywhere. I waved to all the slower boats as they sailed slowly past. They waved back. I called my brother, Steve, who promised to come get me, but not until the next morning. I called Michael, who keeps a big fancy cabin cruiser up the Sacramento River. He laughed at me and told me to calm down.

As the sun set Dura Mater and I settled in for the night. I threw my danforth anchor out and turned on the anchor light. The depth finder read 4.1 feet and I believed it. I boiled water for noodles, heated up my spaghetti sauce, had half a chocolate bar for dessert, then brushed my teeth and turned in for the night. I will confess to being a little rattled, but what could I do? Surely things would look better in the morning.

I woke up in my VBerth when I fell sideways. Huh? Dura Mater, lodged in the mud, was heeled 25 degrees to port. I crawled over to the open companionway and looked out. The world was on its side at 1:15 am Sunday morning. The water lapped gently against the hull, there were a gazillion stars, and the ½ moon lit up my cabin. Hello, Moon!

I could see Channel Marker #21 blinking green in the darkness and a gentle breeze blew the smell of manure to me. And then, what is this? I heard the cows calling to each other in a field just the other side of that nice deep channel. Well, nothing to do about it. I repositioned my sleeping bag ninety degrees so I could sleep with my head elevated in the v-berth and set my alarm for the start of high tide at 5:30 am. Goodnight, Moon!

When I woke up, sure enough the world was straight again. I boiled water, made some strong coffee, waited for the boat to float, pulled up the anchor and unfurled my jib. Lordy! Lordy! Hallelujah! There was a gentle Delta breeze and Dura Mater, bless her heart, sailed by jib alone into the nice deep channel, 'round Channel Marker #21 and slowly up the San Joaquin. After a bit the ebb started again and we motorsailed the rest of the way to the Stockton Sailing Club, where people were slowly recovering from the race and its celebratory after effects.

Lots of sailors from the San Francisco Bay participate in the Delta Ditch Run. Most of those people are racers and they tend to turn around and go home a day or two later from where they have partied hard at the Stockton Sailing Club. The smaller boats are towed home on trailers. The larger keel boats motor home. Regardless of whether it is an ebb or a flood, there they go, motoring home. They have to be back at work Monday or Tuesday morning. Leaving the Delta under these circumstances might prove an anxious time: Maybe the impeller has gotten gunked up with tule grass, the engine overheated, they've been drinking beer for two days and they're hung over. The race was the important thing and that's all done. The motor trip back from the Ditch Run? Probably not an enjoyable experience.

INTERVIEW WITH BUDGE HUMPHREYS

6.3.18 In 2018 the Stockton Sailing Club offered two weeks of free dockage in Buckley Cove to sailors who participated in the Delta Ditch Run. As far as I could tell, I was the only person who accepted that offer.

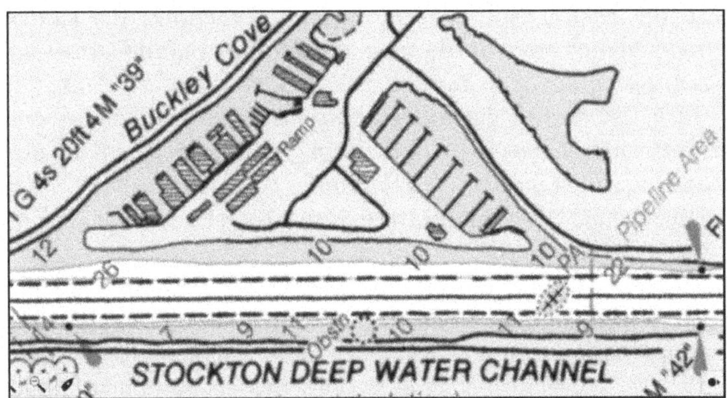

After settling in to my slip on G dock I considered the clubhousc beyond the harbormaster's office. The marina itself is gated to automobiles and across the fairway are new large homes overlooking the harbor, called Buckley Cove. To my city dwelling eyes this club full of sailors seemed incongruous here in the middle of Stockton farmland. How did it happen to be located here?

A day after the race I walked up to the clubhouse and asked to speak with someone about the history of the Stockton Sailing Club, I was referred to Budge Humphreys, a past commodore. We sat down in a corner of the bar there and had a real nice chat. He is a gracious man, Mr Humphreys, a sailor to the core. He's proud of his club, too. Here's what he had to say:

Budge: *We are pretty much the southern boundary of sailing in the Delta. We are one of the oldest clubs in the area that still exists. We started in 1933. The original members of this club went on to become founding members of some of the older [bay area] clubs.*

The Delta Ditch Run, which has become our biggest event, usurped what used to be our biggest race, which was the South Tower race. The South Tower was quite an event. You started right here and you tacked out, starting at 11:00 on the Friday before Father's Day. Sometimes the slower boats, which were at the back of the fleet, wouldn't start until 11:30 or quarter to twelve. You tacked out of here and the river would just be full of boats all the way down and sometimes it was real light [wind] and you spent all day tacking down and you would finally get down [to the Golden Gate Bridge]. The biggest the South Tower ever got was 56 boats I think it was.

It was quite an adventure because boats like yours or mine, the Cal 27s, you get out of here, it would start getting dark somewhere about the Antioch Bridge. So you sailed all night through Suisun, San Pablo. If you were lucky the sun started coming up, you were in San Pablo or if you were real lucky you might get to Raccoon.

The South Tower of the Golden Gate was the original rounding point, but then the Coast Guard said, "No more. You guys can't do that anymore. It's too dangerous." So we started rounding Crissy Buoy or then later, Blackaller, which was originally called Crissy Buoy. The spinnaker ride started from there, not at the [San Rafael/Richmond] Bridge, so you now came back across the Bay and all the way up the River till you got back to this line [he points out the Stockton Sailing Club's large picture window at the San Joaquin River] *and I think the record was right around twenty four hours and that was a very go-fast boat.*

It's arguably one of the hardest races. One year I sailed with two guys on a boat called Third Reef, a Foley one design. Third Reef was the boat that the Hobie 33 was designed after. It was the original boat. It was much lighter than the Hobie 33 but it looked just like it. One of the boats we raced against was called Hotlicks which was a Hobie 33. Sitting side by side they looked almost identical. In their day they were very fast boats.

Both of the two sailors were quasi professional types ... one was a sailmaker, the other was, I think, a rigger? Andre Lacour was one and Tim somebody or other, I can't remember his last name. Those guys both had a lot more experience than any of the rest of us on the boat in those days. We're tacking outa here, we get down to Lost Isle ... Lost Isle's not too far down the river here. We were tacking out and we get there and one of 'em looks over at me and goes "so when does all this tacking end?"

"Another sixty miles." [Budge and I both laugh].

We were the first boat in. Drinking gin and tonics up here in the bar, they both looked at us and said, "That's the hardest damned race we've ever done!"

Your boat, my boat, you're looking at a good run for a boat in that range, the Catalina, Cal 27, 30, was about thirty hours. A not good run would be 35, 36 hours straight. There's no stopping. You were lucky in most of those races if you went down below at all. You maybe got an hour. I did 15 South Tower races. There were guys that did 25 races in the Cal 20s.

In those days I was racing mostly on a Cal 27 pop-top. We had a whole bunch of pop tops. We also had a bunch of the 2-27s in here. Cal was a really big boat at the Stockton Sailing Club. We had a Cal dealer right out in front. In fact, Jim VanDyke, one of our founding members, had the Cal dealership out here. He catered to the Cal boats and a lot of them are still in the harbor. In fact yesterday I sailed the race on a Cal 3-30 here.

It was pretty much, very much a Club Race. At one time only our club boats did it. When we started letting other boats come in from other clubs, that's where the Ditch Run came from. All of a sudden somebody said, "Hey, two weeks before the South Tower all the guys in the Bay are gonna come up and do it."

At first there was only ten or twelve boats from the Bay. They decided they'd all race up here on a Saturday. That was the beginning of the Ditch Run. A gentleman here by the name of Johnny Walker who has now passed away, one of our past commodores, a guy named Pat Brown and John Dukat from Richmond, these guys all came up with the idea of the original Ditch Run.

In the beginning the Ditch run was a feeder race. Well, after the first couple of years of this feeder race the guys decided the feeder race was [Budge starts to laugh]: All downwind? A sleigh ride? Great fun? The Ditch Run was the "fun" part of the South Tower Race. We went down to Crissy Buoy, that's right off the St Francis in the Bay. They wouldn't do it. They wanted the downwind, they didn't want the upwind.

Jackie: Do you think these young people on the Moores ... and the Express 27s ... you don't think they'd do it?

Budge: *Nah. Leave it alone. It ran its course. If somebody wants to revive it and sail from here to the Bay and back then it can be the South Tower Race. People always come up with ideas: "Okay, we'll sail to Richmond and then that'll be the first leg of the South Tower and the Second leg will be the Ditch run sailing back." Yeah. Leave the South Tower alone. It's better for it just to fade away and be the memory than to try to revive it by changing it. If people from here want to race to Richmond before the Ditch run, call us.*

J: So when people say, "I did The South Tower Race", that's a cue, a reminder that there were once people who were tenacious enough to complete such an arduous race!?

Budge nods, a big smile on his face.

J: Coming up river this morning, just outside the Cove, I saw two boats in the mud.

B: *Oh yeah! If you're sailing the Delta and you haven't been aground you either will be or you're not sailing your boat enough. My wife also sails and she's been aground with me. She knows all about it. If I were to call her and say, "I'm aground" she'd just say, "Well, good luck. Did you run aground at high tide?"*

Or "Get in the water and push!"

That's quite often what we do up here in the Delta. My daughter, she was a sailing instructor here for quite a few years. If one of the kids ran aground she'd just jump off her boat and push the kid off the rocks. That's what you do in the Delta. You don't sit around.

Eventually, if you can't get the boat off, somebody just jumps in the water and [pushes] the boat off. We've done that with everything from little twenty footers to 35 footers. Somebody gets in the water and usually if you just get your back underneath it and the guys on the boat get it heeled over some, a good push'll get it outa the mud! Unless you get a particular, rough grounding. Most of the time you're just in soft mud.

The other thing we do is swim anchors out. Probably not coast guard approved. You'll [use] a float cushion, you put your anchor on it, the chain piled up, and some guy tryin' to swim that out ... get twenty, thirty feet at least and then you just dump it off. The people on the boat try to get it to hook and you might have to make two or three attempts at that, but if you can get an anchor off, quite often you can get kedged off and get out of it.

J: That's unique to the Delta because we don't do that in the Bay (laughs). It's so cold!

B: *No! No! In the Bay you wouldn't do it. We've done it midwinter, but then it's not fun. But we also, something that you don't do in the Bay, is in the middle of the race, if there's no wind, people dive off the boats and go swimming. You don't do that in the Bay too often, either. We did Frank's Tract [race]some years ago on a little Cal 27 pop top, and everything just shut down. We threw an anchor out over by the tules across from Owl Harbor and we swam for probably thirty minutes .*

Mr. Humphreys was gracious to the core and generous with the time he spent with this stranger. My impression was of a natural leader and a charming story teller, a man proud of the Stockton Sailing Club and certain of his legacy within it. I thanked him profusely and then he was off to dinner with family and friends.

STOCKTON SAILING CLUB TO DOWNTOWN

6.4.18 Monday morning, the day after my interview with Budge Humphreys, I met one of my Stockton Sailing Club neighbors on G Dock, Bill Miller. Bill told me there was a nice place to eat in downtown Stockton and he was headed there on his beautiful old ketch. Would I like to join him?

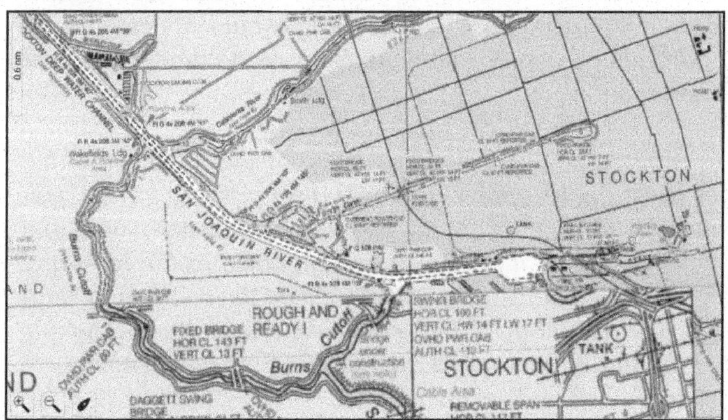

I would, said I, and I had my own beautiful old boat, just here, see? So I followed him up there, my beautiful old sloop following his beautiful old ketch. It was slack tide, and we both raised our spinnakers and ran to the bridge just before downtown, taking them down finally so as to fit through the narrow railroad towers.

We ate lunch at Nina's Mexican restaurant inside a big brick warehouse at the public dock there. There were lots of small businesses in the warehouse but not much activity on a Monday. After lunch Bill Miller got back on his boat and headed down river back to the Stockton Sailing Club.

After an uneventful walk around downtown Stockton I headed back to Dura Mater. At 3:40 pm I raised her sails and we started to sail back to Stockton Sailing Club. The wind had really picked up. It was 18 knots. The wind was right on the nose so I decided not to try tacking through the narrow exit between the covered marina and the edge of the river.

I planned to motor through against the growing flood when ... with no sound at all ... we ran out of diesel. Good thing I could just turn around and go back to the municipal pier. If it had happened when I was under the bridge it might have been scary. The wind is so fluky under bridges, what with the current smacking up against the bridge sides, etc.

Kevin and Matt

I had never used my engine as much as I had on this trip and besides, my fuel gauge was broken. Not that I would have noticed. I had just forgotten all about fuel. Full back in Richmond, my tank was now empty. Who knew fuel could be important on a sailboat? I have learned valuable lessons about the importance of fuel from a sailing friend of mine, Chris Case. Why had I failed to pay attention?

I called Boat US with my brand new membership number, and a very short while later Kevin and Matt showed up in a powerful boat with huge rubber fenders. They shook their heads as they described how they had just pulled a large sailboat off the rocks outside Owl Harbor.

When I asked if I could take their photograph they joked about how they charge extra for photos. But they didn't. I try to be self-sufficient, but as they towed me back to my slip on G Dock I considered how expensive it would have been had I not had that membership.

Once I had tied DM up to G dock I walked up to the clubhouse and introduced myself to Pat Felton, who was sewing himself a new dodger outside under the pavilion where hundreds of people had eaten the night before. Pat seems to be a man who knows everybody, and he referred me to Bob Boomer. "Bob knows engines", said Pat. And he gave me Bob's phone number, which I called.

Bob and I agreed to meet the next day, when he will show me how to bleed my engine, change my fuel filter and start it all up again. After that I'll call a Lyft to take me to the Amtrak station and go home, leaving DM here while I take care of some business back home.

Before the sun went down it seemed that every bird in every tree at the edge of the marina made as much noise as it possibly could make. There was a cacophony of birdsong and then the wind picked up real fast until it was 18 knots. I sat on the bow of my boat and watched the trees, their leaves making that unique sound of branches and leaves blowing violently against each other. Then the wind gradually died down. As I sat in Dura Mater's cockpit and watched the sun go down in an orange sky it occurred to me that there were no mosquitoes.

Richmond Yacht Club had provided breakfast burritos to Delta Ditch Run participants a couple of days earlier. I found mine floating in what was left of the ice. It looked edible to me, so I warmed it in the frying pan on my little stove, ate it up and then settled down with the birds and went to sleep.

6.5.18 The next morning on G Dock in Buckley Cove it was utterly silent at 6:30 am, and I could see the half moon centered in a light blue sky through my companionway. Later in the morning I borrowed a dock cart and walked to River Point, which is across the street from the club property. I bought five gallons of diesel and then watched the action at the dock for awhile.

River Point is a marina with covered slips and a very few end slips that might be used by sailboats. There is a fuel dock here with gas and diesel, and an RV park with at least twenty spots directly on the River and more just inside those spots. There is a community center and an outdoor patio with umbrellas. It's nicely maintained and there's a gate and a guard at the entrance. There's also a freezer full of ice cream bars at the gas dock, inside the small building where they have the cash register.

The people who work at the dock are very agreeable and I have a nice chat with one of the three fellas who work here. I watch as a huge motor yacht comes flying toward the fuel dock. The wind has picked up. The captain is busy steering and yelling instructions to his crew from the flybridge. He has one crew, a very good looking woman who doesn't seem to understand that she is expected to help. The captain yells at the two young men on the dock as he steers straight at it, bow thrusters churning the water at the very last minute to avert impact.

It seems that the captain expects the young men on the dock to throw their bodies between the huge boat and the dock. They're too smart for that, though, and instead they wait patiently, smiling and cheerfully waving the captain away, encouraging him to "try again!" They've seen this behavior before.

The boat heaves away in the wind, and he tries two more times. After a good deal of verbal abuse the beautiful crew figures out that she is expected to untangle the dock lines. The boat gets waved off one more time, and finally, after additional loud instructions from the captain she understands that she is meant to throw the lines to the three young men on the dock, who are standing in a line, patiently, waiting.

The captain is exasperated, the crew's long, expensively streaked hair is whipping across her face, her white Prada sandals are scuffed, but the boat has at long last been tied securely to the dock. It has been quite a show. Peeking into the tiny office I see that it costs $632.80 to replenish this powerboat's fuel tank. Some memories are priceless. For everything else there is Master Card.

DELTA HOSPITALITY

Purple gorilla at Windmill Cove

6.30.18 I left Buckley Cove at 6:24 am and sailed down river to Windmill Cove on Vulcan Island. I was looking for breakfast and instead I found a 13' high inflated purple gorilla on top of a two level cabin cruiser.

After tying up to a well maintained dock behind the yacht I walked around the island. I peeked into the windows of a large building which seemed to be the bar for a huge music venue with tall lights for a stage and an inner harbor with wraparound decking that would hold dozens of boats. There seemed to be no one around. There was a sign declaring the property to be the Delta Water Sports office, but otherwise the island seemed totally uninhabited.

I walked back down to Dura Mater. The only sound was of bees in the bushes. Tied up to the cabin cruiser were inflatable boat toys and two shiny black sea doos. Above the gorilla's head flew an American flag, a flag of the Raider Nation, and a pirate flag, in that order. This person knew flag protocol.

Lisa on her SeaDoo

Then I heard a voice, and walked around to where a woman was looking at her phone on the back deck of the big boat.

I introduced myself to Lisa, whose fiancé, Johnny, is the owner of the boat. They lease space at the dock. Johnny owns 22 Harley Davidson motorcyles and he is racing on this day. Lisa was a registered nurse for years and lives in Tracy now.

She was sympathetic about my search for a breakfast, and invited me to join her and her son for breakfast at Bob's Garlic Brothers restaurant, off 14 Mile Slough between Markers 58/59. I asked about the water depth at Bob's and she suggested we take her sea doo, instead. So I stepped off Dura Mater onto Lisa's sea doo and we followed her son around the corner to a waterfront restaurant nearby.

Breakfast was delicious and I enjoyed talking with Lisa and her son while we ate outside on the patio in the shade. When we were done eating Lisa insisted upon paying. For a stranger and with a $100 bill! $100 bills always impress me. Now that's what I call Delta hospitality.

7.3.18. The day before the Fourth of July I drove from Oakland to the Stockton Sailing Club to check on Dura Mater. Arriving at DM, I uncovered my sail and got ready to leave the dock. Then I remembered that the fuel dock at River Point closes at 5 pm and wouldn't be open again until 9 am the next day. I wanted to leave before then, before it got really hot, so I drove over with my 5 gallon jerry can, came back and poured it into her tank. I also added diesel additive that is meant to deter critter development in the tank. I sure hope it will.

Across the way on Dock G there were four people on a small sailboat preparing to leave the dock. There was a number 26 on the sail. "Ahoy!" I called. They looked over. "Are you racing tonight?" I asked. "No, that's Wednesday night." They were just sailing down river.

Down river. I knew that the flood was at its peak: 4.2 knots against us, the wind 16 knots. But these were Stockton Sailing Club sailors, they who fear not wind and current. The word intrepid came to mind.

They called over to me, "Where are you going?"

"I'm following you!" And I did. They had an outboard engine, and I followed them out the marina, taking care not to unleash the massive power of DM's 11 horsepower inboard.

Once in the channel they raised their sails and so did I. The heat was slowly abating, but I still started to sweat cranking that mainsail up. Pelagic kept me on course right over there toward the trees .

I decided to watch them carefully so as not to become stuck again so soon after my Ditch Run debacle. I matched them tack for tack until, mere increments up the river, I turned around. There were four of them tacking endlessly. I couldn't keep up. Those Stockton sailors. They are something.

AMTRAK TO STOCKTON

7.17.18 After sailing in the Delta Ditch Run I left Dura Mater at the Stockton Sailing Club for several weeks while I flew to Hanalei Bay for the finish of the Singlehanded Sailing Society's Transpacific Race. Back in Oakland, I took the train from Emeryville at 9:45 am and arrived in Stockton at 11:30 am. For a mere $10 I travelled in an air conditioned car, with a table in front of me and the countryside to port. Coffee cost $2 in the refreshment car.

Once through Richmond there are lovely views of the Bay, wetlands, all the communities that are between here and there, right up next to the tracks, all along the San Pablo Bay. Once past the train station in Antioch the fields start. There was a pretty grey shingled home on a platform at the very edge of the Bay, a kayak parked next to its back door.

On the other side of Antioch the agriculture began. Bales of hay filled some fields and there seemed to be a different crop grown every ten minutes of the train ride. There were hyacinth-clogged tributaries, boxes of beehives and vast flocks of egrets flying over the ground and marshlands.

The San Joaquin Street station is a beautiful example of the Mission Revival style of architecture. The building is made of stucco so it's cool inside. Plus it was air conditioned. Once I arrived it cost $12 by Lyft to get from the train station to the Stockton Sailing Club. Easy peasy.

I arrived to find Dura Mater hot and dusty. I was hot and dusty, too, but she'd been sitting in the sun for seventeen days. Poor thing. I learned that bird poop is different in the Delta than San Francisco Bay seagull poop. It is easier to hose off. Now you know.

During my time away Dura Mater's bilge had filled up from a drip at the prop shaft. Every time I use the engine the bilge fills with water. I called over to Ladd's boat yard, across the street from the Sailing Club. Michelle answered the phone and said, "Well, let me ask my guy if he has time to do it, we're putting a boat in the water later today and have a haul out tomorrow morning." When she came back to the phone she said, "Randy says it won't take him long, so come on over."

It took me 15 minutes and two containers of 16.9 fluid ounces of water to motor there from G Dock. I poured one container over my head, one down my throat, and my hair was dry by the time I got there.

Jackie, Randy Landtrip and DM at Ladd's

Randy Landtrip, the mechanic, walked down the dock to greet me. We discussed DM's packing gland and Randy nodded. He said, "Let me just get a hammer", which made me slightly nervous. He told me, "I can do this with my eyes closed."

Dave Russo and son in law Wade @ Ladd's

While I was waiting for Randy to find a hammer so he could smack Dura Mater around, I sat right down on the dock next to two other fellas who were waiting, too. Waiting. It's what we all do in boat yards. The three of us were vying for the limited shade, and we were in a boat yard, so of course we struck up a conversation about boats. Turns out that Dave Russo is from Grass Valley and sails with Dave Cowell on s/v Mas Tiempo. He was at Ladd's to load his 31' sailboat on a trailer to take home to Grass Valley, where he and his family all live.

Dave told me that he has a workshop/airplane hangar, where he works on his boat's rigging and what he refers to as "projects". Dave learned how to sail just four years ago, and now he has what he called the sailing "disease". He also has a smaller boat to sail on Bullard's Bar and some other lake up that way. He has already sailed down to Monterey.

Dave's son in law, Wade, was with him. Wade is a newly hatched sailor, too. He showed me photographs of his two very beautiful young boys, both wearing nautical caps.

Then Randy came back down the dock and descended into Dura Mater's starboard lazarette. We listened to him smacking on something for awhile. Hard smacks.

He crawled out just as easily as could be, and then he

described what he had done in detail: he had replaced DM's packing glands. He gave me explicit instructions and encouraged me to follow them the next time my bilge is filling with water and I am 400 miles offshore. Which is just what I'll do. Ha! As if.

I liked Ladd's yard. The people were real nice. Michelle's daughter worked the front desk of the very well stocked chandlery. There were ice cold drinks and those Mexican coconut popsicles that I love.

Tomorrow my plan is to wake up at dawn in order to sail before it is too hot to do so. The idea is to sail down river past Fourteen Mile Slough , then turn to port past Lost Isle and continue south to Tiki Lagoon, which is supposed to open @ 9 am.

TIKI LAGOON AND LITTLE VENICE ISLAND

7.18.18 The next morning we left Buckley Cove at 7 am under sail. It was a beautiful early morning and there were millions of tacks down river, but the wind was agreeable. It was cool until 9:30 and by that time we had arrived at Turner Cut.

It is such a pleasure to be on a new waterway. I really enjoy not knowing what is around the corner, and also, I sort of enjoy keeping an eye out for the depth. Too shallow there? Okay, over here we go instead. It's fun, and besides, we have towing service! We can afford to be adventurous.

How did we get to Tiki Lagoon? I have no idea. We left the San Joaquin, then passed the Turner Cut resort, which has gas but no diesel, then turned left before the railroad bridge. I learned later that the railroad bridge will open but who knew at this time? I sat at the bar for awhile and chatted with a really nice waitress, Rachel. She has her daughter's name tattooed on her left shoulder: Emily.

Rachel at Tiki Lagoon Resort and Marina

Tiki Lagoon has a newly remodeled bar and grill. There are tables outside, too, which is where I took my two tacos con carne on corn tortillas. Mi favorita. Ice tea served in a tall chilled glass. Mount Diablo can be seen from the tables outside, beautiful and solid in the distance. While I was there PG& E employees came in for lunch, then a party of four and then it got busy. The store downstairs is well stocked in the manner of a minimart.

After lunch my destination was the Little Venice Yacht Club on Little Venice Island. Unfortunately for me, I misread the chart, so I ended up in the weeds. Tried to wend my way in through the tule weeds, ended up in 4' of water but Dura Mater draws 4.5. I know, I know. When will she learn? Well, I was almost ready to call my friends at Boat US when Steve

Robinson moseyed on by driving the robin's egg blue Little Venice Yacht Club motor launch.

Steve Robinson on Little Venice Island

Seems he was on his way to collect provisions when he glanced in and saw DM and me.

"Why, hello there!" He hailed.

"Why, hello to you, too!" I responded, smart enough to not describe the obvious. He is obviously a man sensitive to others' mistakes, and didn't ask if I wanted a tow. He just reached for DM's bowline, which I threw gratefully. He tied it to the cleats on the stern of his own boat.

"Where are you headed?" he asked.

"Little Venice Yacht Club! I've been told that it's a beautiful place." Which was sort of true. Ray Irvine told me that he had visited years ago, on his Catalina 34 Crews Nest.

"Why yes, it is!" he responded, and we were off and around the bend to the correct entrance, which is just inside Little Connection Slough and to the portside off the San Joaquin River. Be careful not to get too close to the point on port, the rip rap came undone during a big storm, or maybe a freighter caused a big tsunami, I forget. Keep the white 5 mile wake buoy close to starboard till you are past the point.

A gorgeous old river boat is supposedly for rent. It has three elegant staterooms, an upstairs lanai, hot tub and huge kitchen with Corian countertops for $600/night. The island can't be reached by car, so you need to call ahead for transportation. What kind of transportation? That isn't clear. I found an outdated website that describes Little Venice Island as a "12-acre exclusive island estate, accessible only by boat ... located on the tranquil California delta." Unfortunately there was no phone number listed.

There are areas all along the waterfront for Adirondack chairs and other seating with gorgeous, unblocked sunsets and views of Mt Diablo. Freighters to Stockton railyards motor slowly past the island, 100 feet from the edge of it. Little Venice Island is a Delta mystery. I think it's a secret.

At day's end I am here in DM's cabin, having received a grand tour of the island, including the various patio areas, the yoga gazebo, the very nice tiled bathroom with shower on the other side of a deep green lawn. It has lots of shade trees which means it is also cool. After a hot day on the San Joaquin River, sitting with a view of the sunset in the shade feels very fine.

7.19.18 The next morning Dura Mater and I left Little Venice Island at daybreak and headed for Owl Harbor.

Back on J Dock Dave Cowell walked over to introduce himself. Dave lives in Grass Valley and owns an Islander sailboat: Mas Tiempo. He keeps it at J dock here in the Harbor. Dave told me about a sailboat race out of Owl Harbor around Mandeville Island, called the Mandeville Run. He is proud to have done the round trip race in 2:06. Then there is another race to Frank's Tract, which starts out on the San Joaquin in early August.

Dave has written about the Delta Ditch Run for Latitude and he wants it to be very clear that there is definitely racing in the Delta. We compare stories of sailing friends we have in common. I call it "boat talk", but really it's much more than just that. It's establishing a rapport by discussing mutual social networks.

Then I walked up to the office and had a chat with Devery. We talked about the business of running a marina, such as the number of slips a marina must maintain in order to stay in business. Owl Harbor has become very popular. She described the progressive interest of a typical Owl Harbor tenant. During the first year, she told me, people come for a week. The next year they come for a month, and finally they just give themselves up to the Delta's charm and reserve a slip for 3-4 months at a time.

There are plans for H Dock to be renovated, replacing and repurposing the existing docks to accommodate the newer, wider boats. Devery says new sailboats have wider beams, and we talked about the way some marinas in Southern California charge per square foot rather than just the length of the dock space. This method of rental takes into account wider boats as well as multi hulls.

She also explained how Owl Harbor uses its threshing boat to clear Seven Mile Slough of the hyacinth plants that clog its approach to the harbor proper. I noted that the wind was light coming into the slough upon my arrival from Stockton, but because there were fewer weeds this year the slough seemed wider and I was able to tack three times and sail into my slip rather than use the engine.

I complimented Devery upon Owl Harbor's beautifully maintained grounds. Every time I visit I notice something new that has been carefully considered for tenants' accommodation. Tenants who drive cars into Owl Harbor must get a code for the gate in order to enter. Bicycles and kayaks are available, but again, only for tenants. Owl Harbor is private and luxurious. I appreciate it enormously.

7.20.18 It's 6:30 am and I wake up with the roosters at Owl Harbor, stumble around for my running shoes. This early in the morning it is cool enough for a light sweatshirt, with shorts. I walk up the wooden ramp to the levee road and run to the channel marker. To my right I hear the voices of men preparing to work in the alfalfa fields abutting Owl Harbor's property.

By the time I head back, with my sweatshirt off and tied around my waist, there are various types of machines and large equipment in constant motion below, moving back and forth in the dusty fields. One day the alfalfa is cut and left spread out to dry in the sun, the next day it is turned over to dry more, then it's packed into bales.

View from Levee Road at Owl Harbor

Finally the bales are piled one on top of the other at one end of the field for further drying in the sun, then they are all collected and taken away.

Every step of the process requires a separate, unique machine. Someone told me that the fields in the Delta accommodate four different crops per year. The number and types of machinery necessary to collect the food we take for granted seems endless. That's a lot of food for tables.

Every time I drive up from the city it seems that fields are freshly plowed, full of small crops, then I watch as the crops grow taller, then finally they are gathered, then the fields sit fallow, then repeat. And then there are the fruit orchards in the Delta, beautifully maintained, the trees trimmed, the rows long and straight, stretching away and seemingly endless.

Back at Dura Mater I open the hatch and feel the light breeze run through the cabin. I fill the tea kettle with water and turn on the single burner stove. Strong coffee starts the day as the heat descends upon us.

INTERVIEW WITH JANET WILCOX

7.20.18 Yesterday I called Janet Wilcox, Bridge Operator at Mokelumne Bridge and asked her if I could come interview her. “Sure,” she said. “Do you know how to get up here?” I assured her that I did, since I had scoped it out last summer, in 2017.

Mid morning on the San Joaquin River it was already 92 degrees. I sailed from Owl Marina to the B&W resort and tied up at the fish gutting table. Before I climbed up the stairs that led to the Bridge office above the Mokelumne River I went to the resort office where I asked permission from Candy Korth to leave my boat at her dock for awhile. Candy’s red surfer bicycle was on the front porch. I knew it was her bike because it had a little plastic license plate with her name on it. She said I was welcome to leave my boat while I interviewed Janet.

Before I climbed those stairs up to the bridge operators office I bought a quart bottle of Langer's pineapple juice from the snack bar. I drank the whole bottle. Anything liquid tastes wonderful in the Delta and that pineapple juice certainly hit the spot. The "bottles are BPA free", too. There I was, standing next to Dura Mater at the B&W resort, re-hydrated and virtue signaling in the Delta. Then I was up the staircase, introducing myself to Janet.

The Mokelumne Bridge is under the purview of Homeland Security. Janet said I couldn't take photographs of the inside of the Operators' Room, and I couldn't even take one of her, which is a shame because she has the nicest smile. Everything is computerized, automated and encased in a large box that looks, Janet told me, like the original from when the bridge was first built.

All along one wall are instruments behind lockers. Janet's work desk is full of Big Buttons labelled with a touch screen above. Very cool. Very high tech. She told me that when the engineers come by to inspect the equipment they are able to categorize and analyze in a heart beat. How many boats pass under? How many times is the bridge opened?

Thc Operators Workroom is clean as a whistle, with a comfortable big old chair covered in a floral print, a standard vinyl office chair and then an extra one which Janet pulled from the corner for me. Windows on all sides, with views of San Joaquin County on one side and Sacramento County on the other. The whole room rumbles when a big heavy truck passes under, but Janet says she doesn't even notice anymore. I could describe it all in more detail but then I might get Janet or myself into trouble, so I won't.

She showed me all the new equipment in the office, and I even got to watch as she opened the bridge a couple of times. It is a remarkable view from up there in the bridge operator's office. The water looks much bluer than it does from a sailboat and the Mokelumne snakes through the farm fields far into the distance.

When I had called her on the phone to arrange for our interview, Janet was curious. She didn't think anybody paid any attention to the Bridge Operators. Why would they be interested in reading about a bridge operator?

I gave her this example, although it was not my own concern: As I was leaving my slip at Owl Harbor one of the full time tenants walked down to ask where I was doing. When I told him that I was going to interview a bridge operator he asked me to enquire about how to get that job. He also wanted to know what Bridge Operators do all day when they're not opening and closing the bridges. So I asked Janet: "What do you do all day when you're not opening and closing the bridges?" Her reply?

"Well, anything at all." Read a book. One fella carves wooden ducks. Then he paints them. She knows this because, when she fills in for him, the desk has paint spots all over it.

Janet has an exercise bicycle in a corner of the room, behind the big control panel box. Bridge operators can't leave the room for the entire shift so she brings her meals with her. That is also the reason for a brand new restroom in the office. On the day I visited she was doing a double eight hour shift and wasn't complaining. We both situated ourselves in our chairs up there in the air conditioned office above the Mokelumne River. I handed the tiny microphone to her, she pinned it to her blouse and I turned on the tape recorder for my interview with Janet Wilcox.

Jackie: Tell me, if you would, a little about your history with the Delta.

Janet: *Oh! Okay! Surely. I grew up in Sonoma County, in Sebastopol. I graduated [from high school] in 1973. I had never heard of Rio Vista. I came to Rio Vista in 1974. When I joined the Coast Guard it was 1974 right out of high school. I was 19 at the time and [the Coast Guard Base] was all new. I met my husband there, in 1975 we got married and we just stayed in Rio Vista. I was the first woman stationed in the Coast Guard Rio Vista, when women first started to be full time. I remained in the Coast Guard for four years.*

Jackie: So you are one of the people who asks us: "What is the nature of your distress? What is your location?"

Janet: *Yeah. My husband knew all the waterways. He went out on the search and rescue, he was the captain [with the Coast Guard]. He was very good at it. We had so many [places] back then. We would even have to go out in the fog, in dangerous situations. It got to be out of control, The captains couldn't even sleep or have any down time because there were so many SAR (Search and Rescue) cases. We didn't have sheriff patrol boats. We didn't have anybody from up near San Francisco coming down, it was just our little unit in Rio Vista.*

Right after the Coast Guard my husband worked at a marina, he fixed the boats, painting and he did bottoms. He was the Boatwright, he actually did the woodwork and the varnish. He was really good at it. So we were right there, close to Delta Marina. We loved the life.

Jackie: I hear that phrase: We love the life up here. What do you mean by that?

Janet: *All the water and the jet skiing and playing in the water and the boat.*

Jackie: You've been here 24 years. Are you called bridge tenders?

Janet: *Bridge Operator. With The California Department of Transportation. It's a state job.*

Jackie: How did you happen to take this job among all the other jobs you could have taken?

Janet: *When I first got out of the Coast Guard I learned how to drive a school bus for the River Delta Unified school District. I drove the big buses. When I went over to the Rio Vista Bridge, I always looked up in that little window. [I thought] how do you get to be a Bridge operator? You know? [Rio Vista] was a small little town. I went down to the maintenance yard in town and [the bridge supervisor said] "I see you driving the bus all the time". He said, "I'll sign you up". I said, "Yeah!"*

You have to study the Coast Guard hand book on regulations and rules. That's what's on the test. I scored high on it. They knew I had been in the Coast Guard, so that was a plus. Dealing with the public. And I'm on the radio with the bus, too. When I was in the Coast Guard I worked in [what is called] the watch shack, where you answer the radio and the teletype. It's similar to what I'm doing here. You are watching and listening on the radio, you're sending the boats out on search and rescue.

So that's what I did in the Coast Guard, then I drove the school bus for nine and a half years. I had to get away from driving the bus, the kids weren't minding and .... I wanted to be a bridge operator. It's kind of a unique job. I have the best view in the world overlooking the river. I'm working for the public with vessel traffic and vehicle traffic. Bridge operators have a big responsibility.

We have to know all the bridges. They all run differently. It's all different hours. We're on call. We fill in when others are on vacation or get sick. Rio Vista Bridge is a 24 hour bridge so they have a lot of graveyard shifts, a lot of evening shifts. The Rio Vista Bridge is the Mother of all bridges for the shipping channel.

Jackie: Do you have bridge operator parties?

Janet: *No. Since we're all one person per bridge and we all have different schedules it's hard to get together. There are so many rotating shifts and graveyard shifts, I don't see those people very often. I'm number 2 on the seniority list, and I've been here for 23 years. It took me that long to get up on the seniority list. We have ten full time operators and 9 part time operators. All the upriver bridges are owned by the State: CalTrans. There's Isleton, Paintersville, Steamboat Slough, Mokelumne Bridge, Three Mile Slough Bridge on 160 and then we have the Rio Vista Bridge.*

Jackie: And they're all different, aren't they?

Janet: *Mokelumne Bridge is a swing bridge, it swings out. It was made in 1941. It's always been a swing bridge. At the time I guess they just figured out that there wasn't enough land in between the water to have them swing it out.*

Jackie: I don't see that many sailboats. Do you?

Janet: *I don't really see a lot of sailboats, no. Mostly speedboats and cruisers.*

Jackie: Have you ever had any bad experiences with sailors?

Janet: *Once in awhile they kinda want to go in when you're first opening it, and they cut corners and they're getting way too close and they could shear off part of their mast. Janet: Once in awhile at the Rio Vista Bridge we have sailboats go through and they want to sail through, and there is this dead spot right where they're going under the bridge and they're flopping like a fish, just sitting there, and they can't get motivated to go.*

There was one situation at the Rio Vista Bridge when I was opening up. He kinda jumped the gun and he went through but his mast got stuck into the bridge. As I kept raising the bridge he was going up with his mast, probably five feet. That was kindof a scary situation. The mast got stuck. There are all kind of eaves and rebar underneath there. I quickly stopped the bridge and he eventually got down. Nobody [ended up] in the water. I don't know if he'll ever do that again, you know?

Jackie: Did it take the mast off the boat or did it lift the whole boat up?

Janet: *It kinda lifted the whole boat up. People are just impatient. They don't want to wait until the whole process goes up, or you tell them how many feet you're going to go up. You know how many feet you need for a vertical lift?*

Jackie: Not really, no. What do you want us to do? Would you prefer that we wait until [the bridge] is all the way open?

Janet: *It's a good idea. It's more safe.*

Jackie: Does it go back the same way or does it go all the way around?

Janet: *It goes out and then it reverses back. We have an open and then we have a close button.*

The Mokelumne Bridge is approximately 13.5 feet above the water. We waited until a tall cabin cruiser approached from the north. The captain called on VHF channel 9 and requested the bridge be opened. Janet demonstrated the steps required to stop the traffic over the bridge. Then she pushed the big buttons that caused the Mokelumne Bridge to swing open and then closed.

Janet told me that, in the Delta, channel 9 is used exclusively to communicate with bridge operators.

Jackie: Do you ever look down there and say, "Gee! It would be nice to be on the water."? Or do you prefer to be up here in air conditioned control?

Janet: *I'd rather be up here. I'm not a fisherman but I just love the sights of the people. I kinda see it as my role as a guardian for the people on the water to be safe. [I] would be the first one, if I saw an accident, to call the Coast Guard. We have a bird's eye view up here. There are a lot of careless boaters out there. There's a lot of boats in one little area here with speedboats and jetskis and wave runners. This is the only bridge that has 20 minute scheduled openings on Saturdays and Sundays because there's so much boating traffic and its stops traffic and traffic could never go because we're opening the bridge.*

We have that every Saturday and Sunday if they call in. They say, "We want that 20 minute opening." 20 after and 40 after the hour. But they still have to call in. We don't automatically open.

I think the ferry has automatically scheduled openings. It's off Ryer Island. River Road goes over across to Ryer Island.

Jackie: Which bridges tend to be the oldest and break down most?

Janet: *Maybe the Three Mile Slough bridge off Highway 160. Have you been up that way? That's an older bridge. That's kind of like the same year as this, maybe 1945. She's got a lot of issues, too. It works differently from here so they all have a different issue. That's a vertical lift. It goes up like the Rio Vista Bridge.*

Jackie: You refer to the bridge as "she"? You said, "she" has some issues. Do people tend to refer to their bridges as female, like boats?

Janet: *I do. I don't know if everybody does. I've been here for a long time. I'm so proud to be here. You know? We work for the public. We're out there in the public sphere even though there's only one operator here at one time. We are on the radio.*

Jackie All you operators are always very civil and articulate and you're pleasant. The sailing people I know are very impressed and we like you a lot.

Janet: *That's very nice to know. It all depends on operators. Some are more grouchy than others. That goes with the territory.*

Jackie: Do they give you customer service training?

Janet: *There's a certain protocol. We're not supposed to argue with the boater or the person on the roadway. Never argue with the boater. Always let them know what is going on, if the bridge is breaking down you try to calm them because lots of times they have to go all the way back around and it's more gas. They really appreciate us giving them the service. It's free and there are so many waterways around here, I don't know what it would be like if we didn't have bridge operators* [laughs]

I tell Janet how appreciative I am personally that the bridge operators in the Delta are so courteous and responsive, willing and able to open and close those massive bridges just so my little boat and I are able to navigate these beautiful waterways.

Janet smiled and said, "I love my job and I appreciate sailors because without them I wouldn't have a job."

We laughed together, then there was a loud click. The tape recorder had turned off after two hours. We talked about our kids for awhile. Janet has three children, two boys and a girl, who are all grown now. We talked about the cost of health insurance and college, and about how cute her son is in the product videos he produces for Sam's Club. Janet was Delta hospitality personified. Then it was time for me to leave and I went to collect Dura Mater before the water got too thin for us to leave.

The sun was high and the sky a bluest blue as I raised Dura Mater's sails. I untied her from the dock and walked her back out carefully, sliding through the mud because it was low tide even for our 4.5' draught. As I motor/sailed DM under the Mokelumne Bridge, two young girls from the snack bar passed on a shiny wave runner and we waved to each other. Janet came out onto the bridge catwalk to wave goodbye, too. It was a glorious day in the Delta.

7.24.18 Living in the San Francisco Bay area one becomes accustomed to organizing the day around traffic. Between 6 am and 9 am, for example, avoiding the Bay Bridge in a car is a good idea. Driving from Oakland to Marin and back requires careful consideration any time after 3pm.

Sailing on the San Francisco Bay is the escape from all that. As long as you can get to the marina and onto your boat you are home free. There are no HOV (High Occupancy vehicle) lanes on the San Francisco Bay, no tolls and no speed limits, at least for a sailboat. Sure, there are no wake zones, where 5 mph is requested, but other than that, there are very few rules for sailors other than starboard right of way.

In the Delta there are many more power boats and sea doos and houseboats than sailboats, than on the San Francisco Bay. Some of the drivers of those boats seem not to know the most basic right of way rules. People who rent boats are not required to obtain boater registration cards, so only people who have a vested interest in staying safe are required to have the cards. What will happen in cases where boats rented from rental agencies collide with privately owned boats? We won't know until something bad happens.

08.11.18 When I arrive back in the Delta by car this time I spread out my old Indian print cotton sheet to use as a sunshade. I bought it on Telegraph Avenue back in 1977 when I first arrived in Northern California, an innocent from Orange County. It blocked the sun in my bedroom back then, and does the same thing years later for my pied a'terre on the water, also known as the Hotel Dura Mater.

Boats with cabins, no matter how abbreviated, remind me of the children's book, A House for Hermit Crab which is about a crab who carries his house upon his back. Except that Hermit is looking for a larger house, not a smaller one. When you move from a house to a sailboat your home becomes smaller and simpler, with fewer options. There is no bad infinity on a sailboat in the Delta.

On DM there's no television, no WIFI. When it gets dark it's time to end the day, and in the morning the coolness and quiet are something to be savored. When I'm at home in Oakland I find myself looking around for ... where is that ... ? Oh, yes, it's on my boat. That lime green paring knife, the purple garlic grown in Owl Harbor's organic garden, the granola that has already been specially mixed with nuts so as to require minimal time and space. Life itself seems simpler.

UP THE SACRAMENTO RIVER

8.12.18 Today's float plan is to sail up the south fork of the Mokelumne River. Or down the south fork. Across the slough the sun is rising, deep orange against the brown fields. But before I go there's that nice run along the levee road of Seven Mile Slough, to the Channel marker 41. The lizards skitter off the gravel trail into the grasses that are so dry they sound like burnt pieces of paper rattling. What do I see sitting up there on top of the marker but that huge blue heron. It's not blue but grey. In the Delta words can be mysterious.

When you stay on your boat in the Delta your whole sailing world changes. First of all, you might be anchored rather than tied to a dock, so no one will wander over to ask about whether you have a particular size bolt or needle nose pliers. Somebody always needs needle nose pliers. What other changes are there? For one thing you can sit around all day in your bathing suit, then jump into the water to cool off whenever you get hot. If your bathing suit is wet and drying on the stern rail it means you can sit around in your underwear while it dries because – why not?

If you are on your boat in the Delta you can do nothing but eat or read or write or listen to music or watch the egret pretending to be disinterested in the fish swimming below it in the water. You can watch it jerk down, spear the fish and gobble it up. That's a real change in scenery from a slip in a marina along the San Francisco Bay.

When you consider the day of sailing ahead of you in the Delta you don't look at the wind first. You can usually gauge the wind by poking your head out of the cabin. What is important in the Delta is the current. Because the San Joaquin is about as wide as is the space between the North and South towers of the Golden Gate Bridge, and the sloughs narrower still. Think about the speed of the current beneath the Golden Gate Bridge and recall how significantly it affects your sailing plan.

Of course, there is a real difference between the effects of current against a long, sleek race boat and a fat little whale enticer like Dura Mater. Dan Wiley once told me that, when faced with a choice between focusing on wind current, his sailing is determined by current. With a lot of hull beneath the surface of the water, current prevails over wind for his Nauticat, the s/v Galaxsea.

In the Delta you might think you're sailing down river when you're really sailing up river, and the sloughs have so many twists and turns that after awhile you have to keep looking at your compass in order to determine whether you're sailing north or south or east or west.

This morning Dave Cowell sees that I have raised DM's sail. He walks down from Mas Tiempo to give us a shove off the dock and she and I are off, sailing very slowly in a gentle breeze. It's not ten o'clock yet.

My garmin handheld is less helpful here than in other places. It doesn't take solid earth into account. Once it wanted to send me straight over a levee, but just in time I saw a freighter that seemed to be plowing across my bow. I realized that it was travelling, not across a field, but down the Stockton deep water channel. Sometimes you might think you see a sailboat moving through the hayfields. The separations of land and water, between levees and tall tule islands, create optical illusions. Delta illusions.

As I approach the exit of Seven Mile Slough I see the Blue Heron again, waiting for me on top of that sunken houseboat with the orange fender that marks its demise. I sail close to the creature and it turns to look at me. Blinks once and then lifts itself away, flapping huge powerful wings, honking in annoyance. Stupid human.

At the intersection with the San Joaquin River there are whole small islands of water hyacinth floating past in the strong ebb. They remind me of the kelp beds off Half Moon Bay that strangled the entrance down there in big swell two years ago.

Although my sail plan was to go up (or down) the Mokelumne River to Georgiana Slough, I make an executive decision and turn to starboard as I exit Seven Mile Slough. Randy of San Andreas Cove Yacht Club motors past us and I call out, "Where are you going?" He responds with a big smile and a gesture to the river ahead, "Out there!"

It takes me until 12:20 to approach Three Mile Slough, which would be embarrassing if I were racing. But I'm not, and there is a little burst of wind for a couple of minutes just off Bradford Island that causes a bit of excitement for about five minutes.

As I turn to starboard to enter Three Mile Slough I raise my Secret Weapon, my pretty blue and yellow drifter. I thought we would be on a beam reach so I had it all ready to go, but the wind isn't cooperating and my executive decision to change the day's float plan has messed up my sense of direction. Will we be approaching the Bridge from the north or the south? I want to sound like I know what I'm doing when I hail the Bridge Operator! I hail the bridge operator on channel 9 with my VHF radio to see whether anyone is there to open the Bridge for us. Sure enough, there's a person waiting in an air conditioned office, responding in that courteous Delta manner.

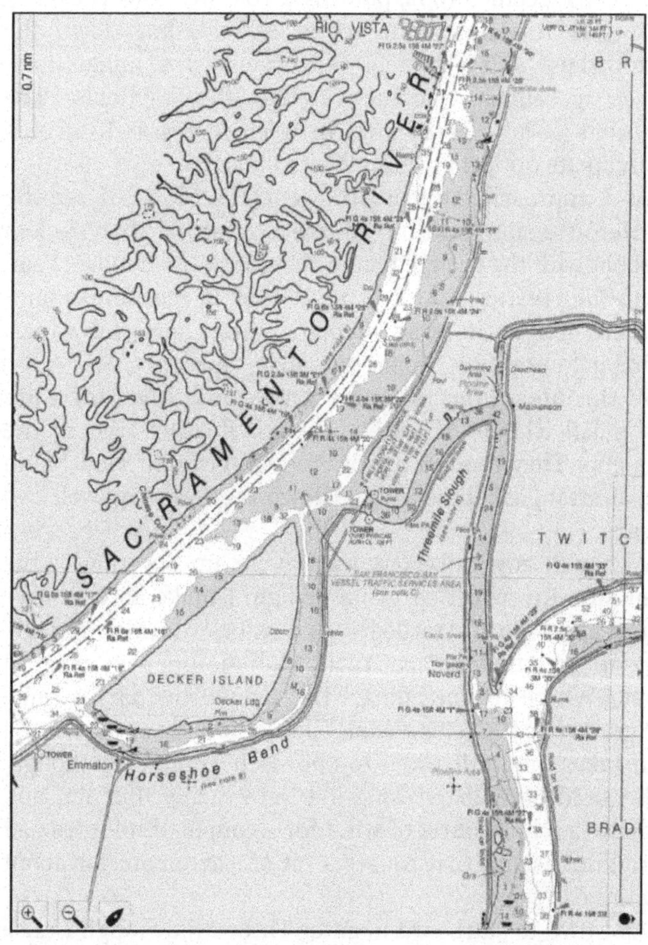

I tell him that I'm coming, that I'm sailing and there isn't much wind, so we'll be awhile yet. He says, "Well, okay then. I'll be looking for you."

It's damned hot. I pour a bottle of water over my head and we slog along until I finally take the drifter down as we approach the Outrigger Marina and Cafe at 1:10.

Outrigger Marina and Cafe

Last summer Chris Weaver was hopeful about this little cafe, but it looks sad today, all boarded up, its docks sagging. I overheard someone at B & W Marina say to someone else that the bank had taken the Outrigger Marina. I've also heard that it's hard to make a living in the Delta.

Once we turn to port 90 degrees I watch as boats launch at the Brannan Island Recreation Area. It's a busy day today, with half a dozen wave runners in formation opposite the launches, lots of squealing by women who think the fellas are going too fast. Old fashioned feminine behavior and everybody's having a good time.

Around another corner, to starboard and there is the Three Mile Slough Bridge, through which we get to the Sacramento River. So I call the Bridge Operator and he remembers us and raises the bridge. It's like a miracle, picking up the radio, hailing channel 9 and a huge bridge rises and falls for little DM and me. I thank the operator, he says "You're welcome" and hangs out the window to wave. That's the Delta for you.

Now Dura Mater and I are on the Sacramento River, in a building flood. The wind is behind us so I raise our Secret Weapon again because I'm too hot to run more lines or go forward to attach the topping lift for the spinnaker pole.

This time the sail combination is perfect. The huge Blue and Yellow drifter performs its role as jib to DM's main and we're sailing wing on wing in the flood current, the only sailboat on that wide big river.

Wing on wing up the Sacramento

All along the Sacramento River to our port side are dozens upon dozens of families, each family with its own sandy beach, approximately every 50 feet or so.

Families picnicking along the Sacramento River

Parents are passing out food to their children from picnic baskets and everybody is sitting under brightly colored cabanas and umbrellas and even a large parasol. They all seem happy as clams as they watch their little kids bobbing around in rubber floaties and inner tubes. It's a hot Sunday in August along the Sacramento and this is a very appealing and free pastime for lots of folks.

I know for a fact that the water is fresh and warm and it must feel cool and wonderful. I think seriously about jumping off Dura Mater but the flood is just too strong and that wing on wing business is working mighty fine.

DELTA MARINA

Dura Mater at the Delta Marina

Lickety split we're at Delta Marina, where I tie up at the Point Restaurant and stagger into the air conditioning. Iced tea! My kingdom for an iced tea! So they bring it, and a crab louie salad, too.

After my early dinner I check in at the marina office. Here we are, Dura Mater and I, tied up for the night in this very protected marina with electricity and excellent wifi, after a hot shower. $27 for the night @ $1/foot, thank you very much. I have done my best to contribute to the Rio Vista economy. Tomorrow night it will be noodles and cheese to average out the extravagance.

INTERVIEW WITH ALAN KLEE

8.18.18 Delta Sailing School is located on Bruno's Island, across Seven Mile Slough from Owl Harbor. It is a private company. Alan Klee and I sat in the classroom of the school in air conditioned comfort while the day sizzled outside.

The classroom has sliding glass doors along one whole wall, big windows, a big screen tv, and a huge detailed chart of the Delta on the wall. Alan, the owner of the school, is a sailor and a natural story teller. Here's what he told me.

We wanted to start a sailing club [on Bruno's Island], myself and a friend. We both loved sailing in the Delta. We figured out that we couldn't really do a sailing club without a sailing school. Cuz most of the people that came to us, they hadn't been sailing before.

First I called up US Sailing and said, "We're just starting a sailing school, we'd like to get certified."

They asked, "When did you start your school?"

"Last month."

"Call us back in two years," they said. "You have to be in business for two years before you can go through us. Just call us back in a couple of years." [Alan laughs, I laugh]

I had this list, you know? US Sailing is a non-profit and ASA (American Sailing Association) is a for-profit. As it happens I called US Sailing first. I didn't know the difference between either of them. If you want to give certifications to your students, from my point of view, being in the business without any kind of certification is a little more difficult. Then I called up ASA and they said, "Well, yeah! Send us a check and we'll put you on the list of schools but you have to have certified instructors."

"How do I get certified?"

"Come down and take our instructor certification course."

Within a few months myself and my partner were both certified instructors. So they made it easy. We went to the certification clinics, got certified and then okay, now we need captain's licenses to get legit. To take passengers for hire on a boat you need a captain's license. Technically the students are passengers for hire.

Alan Klee, founder of Delta Sailing School

Down in the Bay we found three Capri 22s for a total of about six grand. This is a good boat for this purpose. It's easy to sail, it's very responsive. Relatively inexpensive. This was in the early 90s.We figured we were both pretty good boat worker-type people because we had owned boats for years. We figured, if we bought an older boat, replaced the standing rigging, the running rigging, the sails and the outboard motor, fixed all the deck hardware that was old, worn, it's like a new boat except it just looks beat up. Students are gonna beat 'em up anyway. [We both laugh]

I went to the Maritime Academy and did their class there, it took like a couple of weeks and it cost about a grand. I got my captain's license and that is when my partner kind of slowed down. He said, "You know, I think I'm gonna move to Texas." At that point we really didn't have much of a business. He bought me out.

Here at our dock we can do anything as long as we're not polluting, getting stuff in the water. We can't do haul outs, we gotta take it to a boatyard. To Ladd's. Up here Ladd's will let you do your own work. Alan owns Ladd's boatyard, Randy works there. Both of them have been around forever, they know everything about boats. Everything. They are really good at fixing boats.

Alan gestures toward a floating dock next to the classroom. Somebody gave us that. It had been tied to a piling next to the Rusty Porthole [bar and grill] for months. It's 20 x 20. So we went over there to Bethel Island, had lunch, sat around until about one o'clock, four of us jumped in a friend's Catalina 30 and started towing it. We thought, "This is gonna be really easy." From Bethel Island we had to go around Frank's Tract down False River to Fisherman's Cut and then up the San Joaquin to Seven Mile Slough.

We're towing it with a 30' sailboat, he's got it floored and we're going all of about two knots. Once we got onto the River there we were going against the tide, gps was 0.6 knots [he laughs, I laugh]. We got here at ten oclock at night!

We're here! We thought it was going to take us a couple of hours. We had the dock! We had our houseboat!

Delta Sailing School is insured. I'm a retired engineer, my wife is still working. I'm here to have fun and go sailing a lot.

After my interview with Alan I considered the people I have met in the Delta since I first arrived in 2017. People work hard here and it isn't a pretentious place. There is a slower pace of life, too, in stark contrast to the Bay Area, where everything moves more quickly: The traffic, people's physical movements and the cadence of their conversations. It's grounded and my impression is that people who live here are, too.

In the Delta people are working at daybreak and lights go out shortly after the sun goes down. And because of the California climate, harvests are year round. It seems as though every time I drive my car back and forth from Oakland to the Delta the edges of rivers and sloughs are dotted with parked cars and people are fishing from patio chairs or just standing by the water with fishing poles in their hands. It's so very rural compared with the San Francisco Bay area in general.

Owl Harbor to Pittsburg Marina 4:35 am – 8 am motorsailing

8.26.18 You may have heard that it is an unpleasant experience to return back to the San Francisco Bay from the Delta, and this may be correct. Certainly my return trip was unpleasant aboard Dura Mater. Here is my story of our second return, in August of 2018.

Although I remembered getting very wet while returning to the San Francisco Bay in 2017, in 2018 I experienced sailor's amnesia and decided that it couldn't have been that bad. I had no choice but to try again.

I did the smart thing this year and asked Jonathan Gutoff's advice. Jonathan never tells me what to do. Instead he tells me about the circumstances under which he has experienced successful returns. Wait for a good weather window, says Jonathan, and head for home in a flood on a day when there is not supposed to be a lot of wind.

Jonathan has done this many times. He and Christine have gone back and forth to the Delta many times. Now Jonathan is thoughtful and smart in general and he is particularly smart and thoughtful about the trip home to Richmond from the Delta. At this point in my story, recall that pithy parental reprimand from your childhood: "Do as I say, not as I do." Because of course, I ignored Jonathan's advice.

I wanted to stay as long as I could in the Delta, so I waited until friends about to arrive from Wisconsin informed me that, when they arrived they would love to ... sail to Angel Island on Dura Mater! And they were arriving in two weeks!

“Oh, sure!’ I responded.

“I am looking forward to it!” said I enthusiastically.

Then I checked out the Tide Tables in my little free app ***Deltaboating.com*** for the upcoming week. Oh, dear. That didn't look good for a returning sailor: There would be powerful ebb. There would be a lot of wind.

What did it say about the following week? Oh, dear. That didn’t look good, either: There would be powerful ebb. There would be a lot of wind. Okay, then. It was going to be that way. Friends were coming. Dura Mater and I needed to get home.

So there we were, DM and I, motoring out of Owl Harbor into the San Joaquin River before the sun rose. It was real cold that early, and beautiful on the water - in a stark, it's really, really dark and kinda scary sort of way. I was wearing my wool hat and a thick down vest under my foul weather jacket. The air was crystal clear, which made it easy to see the dozens of channel lights blinking red and white and green on into the distance, and there was no traffic!

As the sun came up there *was* that one big ship that snuck up behind me from Stockton, but he hugged the levee and I had noticed him *almost* right away. It is always a good idea to notice huge ships in the vicinity. There wasn’t much wind yet and the water was calm. We were moving along under motor in the ebb tide, well past Bradford Island.

Big Ship in the Delta

When we got to the East Reach the water flattened out briefly as the sun came up and the world was immediately warmer. Starting off the day in layers, I started to shed clothing and switched out my wool hat for a sun hat. Then the wind quickly increased and it was time to shorten sail.

I approached a big huge ship parked at the Military Ocean Terminal Concord, aka MOTCO. I thought I could reef Dura Mater's mainsail in its lee, which made sense at the time. Just as I lowered the mainsail the wind really kicked up – WHAM! - and the waves began to bash us around. Yikes. Hurry on over there! It wouldn't take but a minute to reef, I thought. I careened to port in a semi-out-of-control-way with my mainsail at half mast.

That was when a boatload of military men in uniforms came out of nowhere on their big fat boat with their big fat guns and their big fat, loud bullhorn. They were next to me in no time at all and very effectively communicated that I was expected, in no uncertain terms, to get the hell away from their ship.

There I was, having forgotten to bring my ski mask up from the cabin, with the waves smacking me in the face so much that I could barely see them. Pelagic was complaining loudly that the combination of wind and waves was proving difficult, the mainsail was flapping and the reefing lines were smacking me in the face. What went through my mind? First and foremost?

"At least it's fresh water!"

Then, for the first time ever, Pelagic informed me:

"I'm trying as hard as I can, but this is just too much for me, I need you to hand steer!"

So I hand steered, standing, with my mainsail half down but not yet reefed The military patrol had backed off when I lurched wildly away from them, but they were still watching me through their binoculars. I grabbed my handheld radio and snarled, "Alright! Alright! Give me a minute, willya?" I could imagine them looking at each other and wondering:

"Should we just shoot her?" But they didn't.

By that time DM and I were past them anyway, with the poor mainsail flapping and flapping, sounding very unhappy. Then, instead of unsheeting the main, I heeled hard to starboard and careened almost into the weeds while doing a terrible, sloppy job of reefing. It was better than before, anyway.

As we turned to port, around the corner into Suisun Bay I congratulated myself. Finally you've managed to reef in big wind. What a relief. And then? BAM! In Suisun Bay proper it just got worse! The waves became bigger and closer together, the wind was rattling the rigging, shaking the whole boat, and we weren't making any way at all. In fact, we seemed to be going backward sideways.

So I did the reasonable thing, the honorable thing, the only thing, and spun around hard. In mere seconds, with the wind behind us pushing one way and the ebb shoving us the other way, Dura Mater and I limped into the wonderful, beautiful, relatively calm Pittsburg Marina. The harbormaster at the fuel dock eyed us as we pinballed ("Bink! Bink! Bink!") then smacked our way into an empty slip and I jumped off to tie us securely to the dock.

I was drenched and a bit shaken. Looking over at the fuel dock, I saw that men were watching as I sat there collecting myself. Sad to say, but my sailing mishaps have provided a good deal of entertainment to people over the years. After a bit I walked over to the harbormaster. I asked him if I could park Dura Mater there for awhile, rest up and wait for the water to calm down a little.

"Sure," he said. He told me that the day before it had been windy in the Reach, calm around the corner, the opposite of this day's wind.

"Huh," said I. Then I walked up to the restaurant right there at the marina where I sat in the window and recovered with an English muffin and unlimited coffee. It was 8 am.

Looking at wind reports later, I saw that it was a big ebb and the wind in Port Chicago Reach during that time was as high as 25 knots. Returning from the Delta? It's all in the timing.

I hung around and changed into dry clothes, put the wool hat back on and started out again at 11:20 am. Before I left I walked over and introduced myself to two young people, Sunny and John, who were looking very determined. They had sailed to the Delta out of Berkeley Marina on a Cal 20 with no engine and were planning to head back to Berkeley. Oh, dear. I wished them well. Poor things. I wonder whether they ever made it?

The total moving time from Owl Harbor to Benicia Harbor was 6.44 miserable moving hours, a total of 34.5 nm. Maximum speed for Dura Mater with her Engine by Dave in the ebb was 8.4 knots, an average of 5.1 (miserable) knots.

8.27.18 The next morning I left Benicia Marina at 6:30 am, and arrived at my new slip on E Dock in the Richmond Yacht Club harbor by 9:45 am. It was good to be in Dura Mater's new home, unscathed following an eventful trip.

When I mention that I have spent two summers now in the Delta, people come clean. They admit, "I love the Delta" and get this look of longing on their faces. When pressed they come up with a memory: of being at anchor, just for one night, or swimming in warm water from their sailboat tied up to a tree.

Maybe they remember a summer with their parents and siblings twenty, thirty or even more years ago. They talk about the warmth of the water, the congeniality of the people who live there. It is so different, they say, from life in the Bay Area. And indeed it is.

That's what I am trying to capture in this book. The memories of the Delta which cause people to get that look on their faces. The sense of otherness that they are able to recall for a minute or two while sitting in an urban environment.

I live in Oakland, a block from College Avenue near Broadway, and it is most definitely an urban environment. People park below my bedroom window and walk to popular restaurants in the neighborhood. They park while visiting their dentist or collecting their doggies from the veterinarian office a block away.

Where I live in Oakland it is close enough to the San Francisco Bay so that car windows must be wiped dry almost every morning, close enough to Fire Station #8 for us to hear the sirens as engine cars leave the station. Returning from the Delta my neighborhood seems unnecessarily loud. Does that person need to talk so loud as he walks past my kitchen window? Why don't people in their cars ever stop at any of the four stop signs below my work room window? It is not like the Delta in Oakland and sometimes it is hard to return. But I suppose I must, so I do.

SUMMER THREE 2018

This was Dura Mater's third trip to the Delta. Before leaving from Richmond I spent an afternoon removing Ocean Racing equipment borrowed from friends. Off came Carliane's EPIRB and maps, Tom's storm jib, Greg's 50 watt solar panel and the radar reflector.

Under the umbrella in the San Pablo Bay

I removed the down sleeping bag and jacket, the long underwear, wool hats and socks. I wouldn't need any of that where we were going.

I also had lots of food left uneaten by my Belgian tactician, Philippe. Lots of food. Organic dried fruit. Freeze dried meals and Swiss Miss hot chocolate with tiny marshmallows. Fourteen gallons of water and lots of chocolate. Off it all came. All but the water and the chocolate.

Back on came the mosquito netting, a new chart plotter to replace the third one I broke, sunblock, tshirts and shorts, a new tube of toothpaste, sun hats and sunglasses, my beach umbrella and the pretty yellow and blue drifter.

Richmond Yacht Club – Vallejo Yacht Club 18.9 nm.

7.17.19 This year I decided to take my time getting to the Delta. First I would sashay over to the Vallejo Yacht Club. As a newly minted member of the Richmond Yacht Club, I would seek reciprocity (read: Free) from yacht clubs along the way. Once past the Brothers I poled out the jib and set up the beach umbrella. Staying under the umbrella was pleasant and almost made up for the accursed flies, but only just. We sailed uneventfully over the long hot San Pablo Bay.

A huge pelican dive-bombed into the water behind Dura Mater all the way across. It caught a fish almost every time it dove, that fat show-off. Gybing the mainsail as we turned to port into Mare Island Strait we were on a beam reach all the way to the Vallejo Yacht Club harbor entrance. I decided to test drive this reciprocity business and called ahead to Debbie at Vallejo Yacht Club.

"Sure," she said. "Come on over. There will be Wednesday night races but there should be room at the guest dock." And there was.

We left Richmond Yacht Club Harbor @ 10: 30 am and arrived @ Vallejo Yacht Club with plenty of time to spare before the Wednesday night buoy race. Our moving average across San Pablo Bay was 4.7 knots, and we rode the flood the whole way. I have resolved to savor my arrival in the Delta every year, so there was no hurry to arrive.

I abandoned Dura Mater long enough to ride along on Jack Vetter's zippy J80 Pearl in the Wednesday night race around RG N "BP, the buoy at the base of the Carquinez Bridge. Jack Vetter and his crew Michelle, Kimball and David were an impressive team, but we lost to a Melges by mere seconds.

Dura Mater was tied up to the guest dock, so after pizza I climbed aboard and slept for eleven hours. Sailing all day and socializing with racers is hard work. I was also waiting for the ebb. At noon when I raised sail there was a strong wind that pinned DM to the dock. Three members of the club readily agreed to help by pushing her bow out and @ 12:40 we began another beam reach down a windy Mare Island Strait.

Vallejo Yacht Club to Pittsburg Yacht Club Harbor
12:40 – 5 pm , 21.8 nm

7.18.19 As we exited the Strait and turned left we sailed under the Carquinez Bridge where there was a immediate change in both the weather and water. The choppy waves of Mare Island strait smoothed out and I shook the reef from Dura Mater's mainsail. We continued through the Carquinez Strait, under the Benicia-Martinez Bridge, mindful of the channel markers as we progressed through the Bull's Head Channel. Our moving average was 5.1 knots upriver on a flood, a beam reach almost the whole way.

The wind built through the afternoon, as wind tends to do, especially in Suisun Bay. As we approached the turn into New York Slough the wind became down right impressive. At 5 pm DM and I were happy to turn into the first entrance to the Pittsburg Marina, where the Pittsburg Yacht Club is located. There is a sign at the entrance: Private. There are two parts to the Pittsburg Marina, each nicely maintained, but DM and I were interested in the reciprocity/free part.

The members of the Pittsburg Yacht Club were very friendly and the clubhouse is beautifully managed. Reciprocity was extended to me but the marina is still run by the city of Pittsburg so my slip cost, in 2019, was 50 cents/foot. That seemed a small price to pay to be right there at the club, with its classy hot showers at the end of a sweaty day in the sun. Thank you to Sharky, a pretty blond woman who also gave me the Club WiFi code. I was told that the second night is free, even upon your return back from the Delta, but don't quote me because I didn't see it in writing.

The next morning I walked over to the other side of the Marina, not a long walk, and ordered a breakfast and coffee @ the restaurant near the harbormaster's office. I called fellow singlehander Mike Cunningham while I had a second cup of coffee. Mike lives in Discovery Bay with his wife Jacqueline and his boat Jacqueline. Jacqueline and Mike have a dock and a deck and we were invited to both, so that was the destination. But first: How did we get there?

"Stand by," said Mike. He put me on hold while he looked up the chart on his iPhone. I planned to anchor out along the way, so I asked him for a recommended anchorage.

"Anywhere, especially along False River," Mike told me. He sent me this email:

"Once under the Antioch Bridge, it's approximately 5 nm further, then turn to starboard at False River, staying close to the rip rap. This is where you start to use your depth finder."

Farm along Old River

From the Pittsburg Yacht Club harbor we sailed along with Martinez to starboard and on to the San Joaquin River. Then we were under Antioch Bridge. There was a pale blue sky on this day, and just enough wind from the northwest for Dura Mater to coast along under spinnaker at 3.3 knots in the slack tide

Between Pittsburg and the Antioch Bridge there are industrial properties to your right and tule islands to your left. Once past the bridge there is green, low lying farmland, and sky as far as the eye can see. The change in landscape is remarkable.

As long as you follow Mike's directions closely, keep an eye on your depth finder and if your chart plotter tablet doesn't die, you'll be fine. If your chart plotter battery dies, as mine did, you may decide to stop right there and anchor in a mess of tules in order to reconnoiter and maybe even stay the night. I taped Mike's directions to Discovery Bay to DM's companionway, just below the depth finder.

Sailing down Old River toward Discovery Bay I decided to anchor when my chart plotter ran out of juice. It was too hot to keep sailing, the wind had really ramped up, and I was sweaty and hungry. Of course, by the time I was anchored I was even hotter and hungrier and besides, I'd used up all the bad language in my repertoire. So I just gave it all up for the night. I turned to port just below Rhode Island, a tule island west of the Holland Tract, in the middle of Old River. It is east of the Bacon Levee Road.

"Time to recharge the chart plotter and try again tomorrow," said I to my crew. It would be a new day with new language.

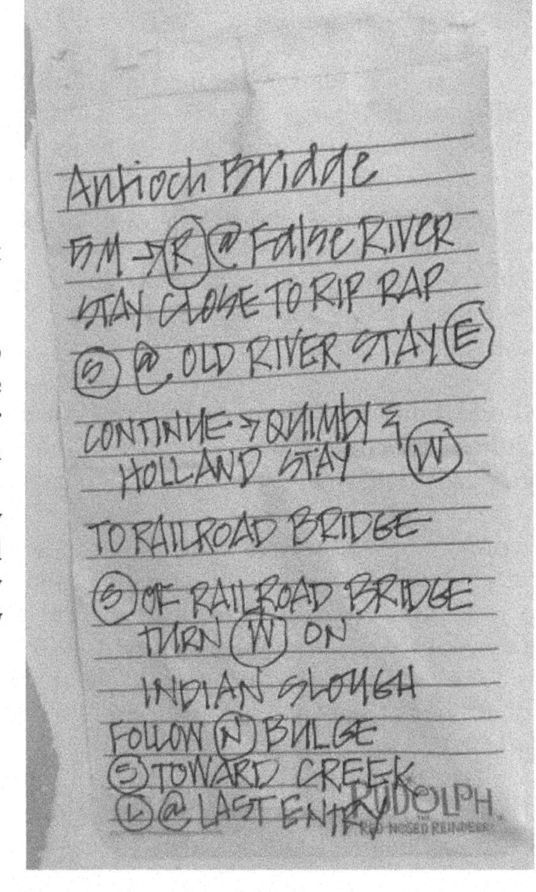

Pittsburg YC Harbor to anchorage just below Rhode Island 21.3 nm, 5 hours, 35 minutes Average 3.81 knots.

7.19.19 I dropped my aluminum spade anchor @ 2:07 pm in 14.1' of water and 16 knots of wind. Once anchored I saw that it was still 79 degrees at 7:30 pm. There were no trees to block the wind and it sounded like thousands of birds were out there, clinging to the hard stem tules, as they thrashed around in the wind. They squabbled with each other loudly as I heated up leftover Mongolian beef.

I drank four bottles of water, climbed into the v berth and tried to sleep. It took me awhile to relax. It was so windy that Dura Mater was being pushed sideways. This was my first time anchoring in wind. Had I done it right? I sure hoped so, but if not I would merely be shoved into mud on the other side of the slough.

What is a tule? According to Merriam-Webster it is "either of two large New World bulrushes". Tules are bulrushes that grow in marshy lowlands or swampy land. They are beautiful when they sway in the wind. During that first night anchored, the sounds against the boat were like sounds you hear outside your tent while backpacking. Small animals snuffling, maybe a coyote in the distance. Here? Were they wolves? Probably not. Pythons? Now that seemed much more plausible.

Rhode Island Anchorage to the Cunningham Yacht Club in Discovery Bay = 2.5 hours under sail, then one hour under Engine by Dave. 9.91 nm, 2.9 knots average.

7.20.19 It was really windy during most of the night, but my spade anchor held beautifully. In the morning I tried to raise anchor with my sails up. This was a mistake. Dura Mater wanted to get going before the anchor was up fully, so we were moving sideways out of that anchorage while I was still up on the bow and before I could scramble back to the cockpit.

The anchor came up dense with mud and tule grass, both of which are heavy. Of course it made a mess of everything, which was another lesson learned.

I was prepared in a couple of ways because I had listened to what Jim Quanci told me about anchoring his Cal 40. Green Buffalo's skipper carries several big towels for anchoring and an extra pair of gloves for pulling up the chain. "And remember to put them on!" he said. "Otherwise it's hard on your hands."

He also told me that the gloves get so muddy, this is what you do next: Put a piece of line through the fingers and drag the gloves behind your boat for awhile to wash the mud out. They will dry in 1/2 hour in the Delta heat and then you're ready for the next time. Thanks, Jim.

Bascule Bridge over Old River

Look at your Delta chart and find the railroad bascule bridge which is over Old River just south of Bacon Island. Is it not the coolest thing? I called on VHF Channel 9, a real nice woman responded, and I asked her if she would open the bridge for me. She said, "Sure, but turn on your engine."

"Yes, Ma'am," I replied, and started my engine. The Bridge opened as if I'd said 'Open Sesame' and then we were on the other side of it.

Just a bit past the Railroad Bridge, as I turned into Discovery Bay from Indian Slough, the wind was on our nose, so I furled the jib and dropped Dura Mater's mainsail.

Indian Slough sign

There was a No Wake rule once we entered Discovery Bay. DM and I enjoyed reverse rush hour. It was a Saturday morning and there were dozens and dozens of power boats exiting Discovery Bay with at least four people aboard each. Discovery Bay was a spawning area for sea-doos and ski boats and all kinds of zippy water rides. They kept shooting out of the exits into Indian Slough. The wakes were incredible. I felt like a junior dinghy sailor being passed by a row of fast ferries in San Francisco Bay.

It took me 3.5 slow, luxurious hours from my anchorage below Rhode Island to get to Mike and Jacqueline's place. The last hour was spent poking along under engine against a stream of power boats full of women in bikinis.

Yes. There are a lot of bikinis in Discovery Bay and women inside 'em. I just hope they wear gobs of sunblock or else they're going to get really sunburned because those bikinis are very small.

There aren't many sailboats in the Discovery Bay community. I counted only five in the whole place, and I motored around casing the neighborhoods for about an hour trying to find Mike's dock. He had given me his street address, which proved particularly unhelpful. It was fun to see all the highly polished cabin cruisers, trawlers, power boats, ski and cigarette boats.

Arriving by water, my impression of Discovery Bay was that it is similar to a brand new Venice except that the villas are not crumbling into the water. Instead of vaporettos there are powerboats. Every house has a dock and almost every dock has at least one or two boats. Nice boats, too. These are not cheesy floaties. Discovery Bay is kind of swanky.

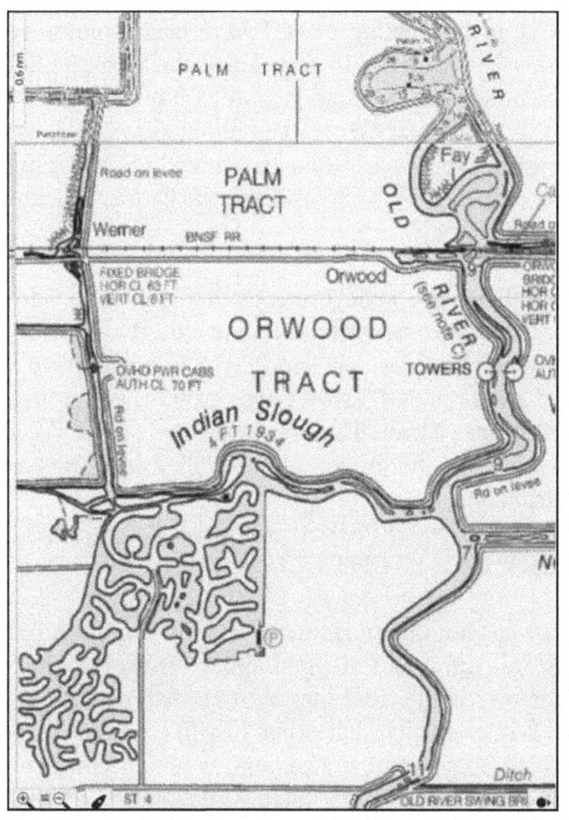

I arrived midday Saturday at the Cunningham Yacht Club (CYC), also known as the home of Jacqueline and Mike Cunningham. Mike and Jacqueline were swell hosts. They offered up their shower with eight water jets installed by Mike. I found them a bit disconcerting, but I am adaptable. Then we had steak and baked potatoes on their deck overlooking our boats. It was the good life.

Before Mike turned in for the night he loaned me a 5 gal jerry can full of diesel. He wrote ***Jacqueline*** on it in big black marker but I still have it today: a purloined memento of my visit to Discovery Bay.

Post visit I received this email from Mike regarding currents in the Delta waterways:

> "This is an interesting topic I have been pondering for nigh on 18 years since I had a slip at the Stockton Sailing Club. The tide at the Golden Gate is 8 hours out of sync with the tide in Stockton. It is about 60 nautical miles distant (on the river) so I have assumed there is a bubble of max current which travels from the gate to Stockton at about 7.5 knots."

> "When there is a good breeze and I catch the tide just right, I can get on that bubble and ride it almost all the way home. It saves me about two hours. I have seen almost 10 knots SOG [speed over ground] going through the Carquinez Strait. That's fast for my boat [a Freedom 30]. Now, if I catch it just wrong, well, I drop the anchor and drink beer."

DISCOVERY BAY YACHT CLUB

7.21.19 Sunday morning at 7:56 am the Cunningham Yacht Club was quiet as I stepped aboard Dura Mater. I saw another person loading fuel jugs into his fishing boat across the water. We waved to each other just like neighbors do in Oakland. Well, maybe not in Oakland. A blue heron flew low across the glassy water, its huge wingspan spread wide. Certainly I've never seen a blue heron in my neighborhood in Oakland.

Motoring around the Discovery Bay loop, we turned to starboard just before the sea wall and continued slowly all the way down to where there were two signs: One read BarryLand and the other read Barryland Farms. Coasting in neutral I steered toward a tall, handsome fella who was watering a lush lawn designed around a swimming pool which was situated next to a beautiful building. It looked like it might be a small boutique hotel. There were palm trees and exotic flowering shrubs, several patio tables with umbrellas, a cabana and lounge chairs. A huge American flag flew lazily on a tall flagpole. There were slips for about a dozen boats and a long guest dock.

"Good morning!" I smiled big and called out, "Are you serving breakfast?"

The man laughed, a big deep throated laugh. "Sure!" he said, and laughed again. He thought that was really funny for some reason, and I decided that I did, too. So there we both were, me floating slowly by on the water, him watering the gardens, laughing together on this beautiful day with its blue sky in the Delta.

"This is my home! Do I serve breakfast! Ha!Ha!" I realized my mistake. Barryland was a large private estate that I had mistaken for a hotel. I circled around once more, closer in and ever more slowly.

"Oh! So, no breakfast, then? Sorry! Your home is beautiful!"

He smiled BIG, put the hose in the crook of his arm, dipped his head and did that prayer thing with his hands. "Thank you!"

"Do you know where I can get breakfast?"

Even though I was stupid, I was still hungry.

He pointed down between two rows of covered docks, where there was a restaurant, way down at the other end.

"Thank you!" I waved.

"You're welcome!" He waved back, shaking his head, still enjoying the joke.

At the entrance to the fairway there was a long dock, with three fuel pumps: two for gas and one diesel. There was also a ramp for powerboats and sea doos and any kind of trailerable water toy. I motored slowly down past a long series of covered slips that contained Docks A and B.

Beneath the covered slips were large double decker cabin cruisers stacked side by side, and at the end of the fairway was the Boardwalk Grill restaurant with its outside seating. There is a long guest dock for patrons, and it was indeed serving breakfast. But, wait! What was this to starboard?

Discovery Bay Yacht Club

The Discovery Bay Yacht Club has two slips for guests of the yacht club. Dura Mater was the only boat, the only sailboat. We pulled in, tied up and raised our Richmond Yacht Club burgee. I walked around to the huge, impressive front door and tried to open it. It was locked, so I banged on it.

Finally it opened, like the door in the Wizard of Oz, and a fella asked me, “Can I help you?” It was Bill Murphy, a member of the DB yacht club for 38 years.

I pointed to my sailboat in the slip and asked if we could seek reciprocity. And did they serve breakfast? Of course I could have reciprocity. No breakfast, but brunch would be ready at 10 am. Would I like to wait? Mr. Murphy would make a pot of coffee if I wanted to wait. Sure I would. So I sat at the bar while he made the coffee and once I had a cup in hand Bill gave me the grand tour. There were photographs of sailboats everywhere on the walls of every room, but he said they don’t see many sailboats in Discovery Bay. Bill sold his own boat, a Bayliner, last year and moved to the golf course across the street.

I asked if people like him call their boats motor boats and he said, no, they prefer the term "powerboat". I asked him what powerboat owners think of sailboats. Bill admitted that powerboat drivers tend to believe "sailboats are always in the way" which was something that I had suspected all along. Bill assured me that, while he himself understands that sailboats need to tack back and forth in fairways, he does not think this is a common understanding. We talked about all the funny looks I had gotten from people the day before. Bill nodded in appreciation of my dilemma.

He introduced me around the club as an exotic visitor: "She came here on a SAILBOAT!" I sat at the bar, drank Bill's coffee and watched golf on the big screen color television. Brunch was all you can eat and cost $13 plus a tip to the lovely Antonia, she of the big eyes and beautiful smile.

We discussed reciprocity between yacht clubs. Bill and his wife, Fran, travel all over the country, and they seek reciprocity wherever there is a yacht club. He told me that fancy drinks at the West Palm Beach Yacht Club cost only $2.50 each while comparable drinks in nearby restaurants are $9. When he and his wife visited their daughter in Pittsburgh they sought reciprocity at the Pittsburgh Yacht Club in downtown. He noted that there are no boats at all in downtown Pittsburgh and, having visited that city myself, I believe him.

7.21.19 After we left Discovery Bay Dura Mater and I zigged and zagged under sail to Bedroom One, which is off Potato Slough.

I arrived to find several small houseboats and sailboats already anchored. I noticed several men drinking on the back patio of one of the houseboats. They watched as DM and I approached slowly by engine, her mainsail still aloft. It looked like their boats were all anchored right up close to the little island, so I thought I should follow apparent protocol and do the same.

Gliding in toward the island, I ignored my depth finder when it started ringing. I hurried up to the bow to drop my anchor, only to hear the peanut gallery yelling "No! No! Not there!" So I pulled it up again, and we swerved over and away where we bumped (gently, very gently!) up against a beat up trawler that shall remain un-named.

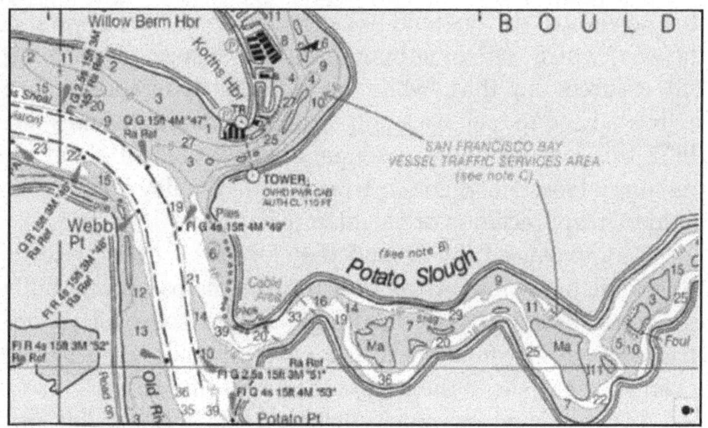

Circling around, I made another run at it and waited until the Peanut Gallery reliably yelled, "NOW! DROP IT NOW", which I did. Well, that was still too shallow, but the anchor held.

After responsibly coiling all the lines that needed to be coiled, I jumped into the water to cool down. While drying off in the cockpit I googled the Delta Loop and learned that Pirates Lair was the staging location for the 2019 Ephemerisle. Earlier in the year a friend had invited me to Ephemerisle, which has been referred to as the Burning Man of the water. I had forgotten about it, but here it was on our way to Owl Harbor.

The next morning was a Sunday. The sun woke me in the V-berth and it was hot already. I don't close DM's companionway entrance at night, preferring to get the cross breeze through to the hatch, and it is reliably cool at night. That means I am warm and cozy in my Coleman sleeping bag, while the nighttime temperature is cool. I drank my coffee and listened to the sound of all the birds on Fig Island while the sun streamed into the cabin.

WHAT IS EPHEMERISLE?

The mission for the day was to find out more about Ephemerisle. Our destination was Pirates Lair, but before leaving the Bedroom I had to deal with all the mud and weeds that came up with the claw anchor.

Tule grass on spade anchor

Raising anchor was an ordeal, and I motored slowly around the island with my anchor hanging from DM's bow, enmeshed in an incredibly dense and heavy mass of weeds. It was so heavy I couldn't pull it up onto the bow, so I let it drag just above the water while Pelagic steered us out of Potato Slough. We drifted slowly under sail past the fisherman and his wife.

They watched as I lay on my stomach on top of the muddy chain and slowly disentangled the weeds from the anchor with my boat hook. It took half an hour.

As we finally exited Potato Slough into the San Joaquin we went aground briefly. Looking over to port I saw a sea lion trying to swallow a big, fat white fish. The fish was so large that the sea lion was gagging, trying to swallow it whole. That animal spat its fish up into the air three times before it was able to get it down. A sea lion with bad manners in the fresh water of the San Joaquin River. Who knew?

7.22.19 It is 1.72 nm from Bedroom One to Pirates Lair and we arrived at 11:47 am. After tying up at the guest dock, I walked up to the cafe and ordered a BLT and iced tea. I had my eye out for people arriving for Ephemerisle. Never having been to Burning Man, I didn't really know what to look for, so I introduced myself to the person ahead of me at the cashier. Danny is a French mathematician who had just spent a year at the Institute for Advanced Study in Princeton. He had come from New Jersey to participate in Ephemerisle. Seriously.

Danny told me that if I wanted to learn about Ephemerisle I should talk with "Crash", who turned out to be the fella sitting at the table in front of the Café. That was Chris Rash, also called Crash, a computer programmer from Silicon Valley, who has been doing the Ephemerisle for a number of years now. Chris/Crash explained that 'doing means organizing, but not really organizing'. He explained that Ephemerisle is a gathering of friends with a shared interest in re-using the earth's resources, sustainability and limited consumerism.

Who else did I meet? Besides Chris and Danny, there was a young man named Quintin with a duffel bag from an Ivy League water polo team, Andreas from Colma, and Robert, a tall man with cowboy boots and a Dave Morris grin. They all looked forward to enjoying the upcoming week on the water with like-minded people. They were waiting at Pirates Lair to be collected by a "boat" and taken to the larger group near Mandeville Island. Chris and this informal group apparently raft up together in Clipper Cove once/month. They call themselves members of the Washed Up Yacht Club. Everyone was very nice.

I donated a tube of sunblock to the Ephemerisle Cause and then stepped aboard Dura Mater as they boarded their own boat, which was a sleek motor yacht with a lot of power. Dura Mater and I were invited to join them at Ephemerisle, but we were on a mission to get to Owl Harbor. At the end of the day, you can't beat Devery's showers, which are nicer and more spacious than those at the Empress Hotel in Victoria British Columbia. This is true. Call me bourgeois.

Pirates Lair to Owl Harbor 4.75 nm 2.9 knot average

7.22.19 This year I have become newly aware of tides and currents here. Yes, it has taken me three years. I am a slow learner. Also I have been distracted by other things: the beauty of the place, the vistas and just being here. I've wandered around.

In 2017 my goal was to simply arrive in one piece at Owl Harbor. In 2018 I sailed in the Delta Ditch Run to Stockton, and this year my initial destination was Discovery Bay, to visit Mike and Jacqueline. Dura Mater and I, we meander. And eventually, when we go to the Delta, all sloughs lead us back to Owl Harbor.

TOWER PARK MARINA

Owl Harbor to Potato Slough 11 am – 1 pm 3.19 nm
2 hours all by sail.

7.30.19 Sitting in Dura Mater's cabin, tethered to "I" dock in Owl Harbor, I open the Delta chart and peruse it. Where will Dura Mater and I go next? Today it is a clear and very blue sky. Using my trusty fishing app to check tides, I decide that today might be the day we find our way to The Meadows.

Instead of sailing directly up the Mokelumne, we'll sail over to Potato Slough, past the Bedrooms, check out that route. We'll visit Tower Park Marina, then continue on up the South Mokelumne. I'm interested in anchorages along that way, too.

There's always a bit of uncertainty to any new destination, though no reason to be anxious. I have a full tank of diesel and more in the jerry can I've stolen from Mike. We also have two anchors that are more than adequate for anywhere in the Delta. So, here we go! The coffee is gone. Granola has been consumed. There is no reason to lollygag.

The cart is missing from I dock, and I need it to transfer the five gallon container of diesel from the trunk of my car to DM. Looking down from the levee road, I see a gaggle of big kids who have commandeered the cart for their picnic food. I go down and ask if someone could help me carry the diesel. Sea Scout Nick volunteers to follow me up to my car. I pop the trunk and he lifts it easily, carries it down the ramp to DM. On the walk down we have a nice chat.

Sea Scout Nick

The Sea Scouts are on a two week trip in the Delta, learning how to sail and navigate. They are based in Aquatic Cove, San Francisco. Nick tells me that membership in the Sea Scouts costs $60/month and there are two adults with them here in Owl Harbor.

"Well, technically they're adults," he says.

"What does that mean: technically?" I ask. "How old is a 'technical' adult?"

"24 years old", is Nick's answer.

I laugh, and tell him that my own son certainly didn't act like an adult at 24. Nick laughs agreeably at that, and I send him off with a ziplock bag of homemade cookies.

As we leave Owl Harbor I see a gaggle of Sea Scouts congregating on J Dock around a motor boat and an older wooden sailboat.

Sea Scouts on J Dock

Dura Mater and I sail slowly out of Seven Mile Slough and once we were in the River I turn around to watch as they come barreling out of the Slough. They had raised a big genoa on their wooden sailboat and were sailing out fast. Until they went aground.

I raise my beach umbrella and set the Pelagic, turn to watch again. The Sea Scouts had lowered their sails, then somehow got their boat and themselves extricated from the mud. They raised sail and began to move again, quite fast and wing on wing. Then they went aground again. They were sure learning a lot about how to raise and lower sails. Or maybe they just got hot and decided to stop and jump in the water. People do that a lot here. I should've just anchored myself and jumped into the water, but I am on a mission. So we keep going, turning to port and head up (or down) Potato Slough.

Potato Slough to Tower Park Marina 1-3:30 pm, 8.1 nm

Dura Mater and I sailed up the San Joaquin River, turned to port at Potato Slough, then followed it around to where it meets up with Little Connection Slough (to the south) and Little Potato Slough (to the north).

Spin up along Potato Slough

I had no idea what the waterways were called at the time because I was flying a spinnaker, which always makes me a little nervous.

Throwing caution to the wind, Dura Mater and I just followed the curves of the water, with me trimming, gybing, trimming, gybing, trimming, just trying to keep up. The sun was so bright it was hard to read the chart plotter, and I kept forgetting which way the slough would turn up ahead, so some errors were made. Ended up either figuring right or sailing sideways on what I have heard referred to as "hot" angles. On this day, it meant that the slough curved that way when I thought it was going to curve that other way.

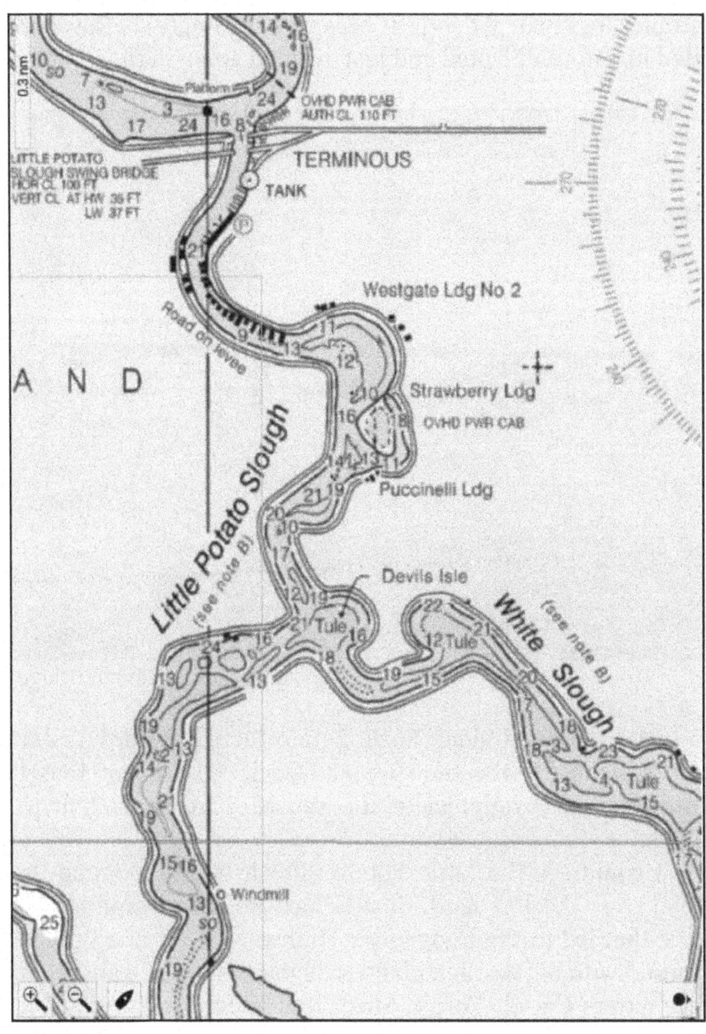

All that moving around was hard in 92 degrees. There was potential for heat stroke just ahead at every turn but I couldn't do more than grab three bottles of water from the galley sink below the companionway.

At the southern end of Potato Slough I failed to turn to port, instead heading straight into Little Connection Slough where I saw what used to be Herman and Helen's marina. It seemed deserted, the surrounding signs mildewed, the entrance less than 5' depth. It became alarmingly shallow and silted in before I pivoted and just avoided going in the mud.

Little Potato Slough Bridge

We continued along Little Potato Slough toward Tower Park Marina. By the time we arrived it was so hot that I almost failed to appreciate the sense of accomplishment. Almost.

I could see the Little Potato Slough bridge looming up ahead over the low land. Just before we sailed around the curve that led to the bridge over Highway 5 we passed sheds adorned with big wooden plaques facing the water. Painted in large letters I read: Turnip Shed. Radish Shed. Onion Shed. Tomato Shed.

Radish Shed at Tower Park Marina

When we arrived at the marina the restaurant was open and air conditioned. Tower Park Marina is a family-oriented place, with campsites and bumper boat rentals. When I was there, on a Wednesday night, there were two large groups of families with kids eating dinner together. I ordered tilapia tacos and iced tea and chatted with the waitresses, who were very nice.

This was 2019 when it cost $20 to launch a boat and ice cream bars were $3.98. There is diesel, but you have to carry it up from the parking lot. Fuel at the waterside is gas only. I paid $35 for a slip for one night and enjoyed the hot shower, but it is hard for a bathroom to impress after bathing at Owl Harbor.

The best part of my stay at Tower Park Marina was meeting Aaron, the resident security guard. During the winter Aaron is a longshoreman. During the summer he commutes from Lodi where he lives with his girlfriend and her child.

Aaron explained to me that the covered boat sheds with the names dated from the early 1900's. Riverboats brought vegetables grown locally to the sheds, which then loaded them for delivery onto the Western Pacific Railroad. Aaron's girlfriend's grandmother, 93 years old, had lived on a boat in Turnip Shed for thirty years. It was only last year when she finally moved into town.

After eating dinner I walked over to his tiny air conditioned office right there on the dock and introduced myself. I asked if the water from the hose was potable, I wanted to refill my water bottles. Aaron told me that it was potable, but I was welcome to refill my bottles from the big filtered water bottle in his office. And it was cold. So I did. I told Aaron that the bridge requires 4 hour notice to open. He was skeptical and said that he had never seen the bridge open at all. Was I sure that it would? I told him I hoped so, because I didn't want to go back the way I had come. Where's the fun in that?

Aaron at Tower Park Marina

I climbed back onto Dura Mater with my water bottles, ready to call and make an appointment with the appropriate authorities for the bridge to open the next morning. It proved more difficult than I could have imagined. Referred to by locals as Tower Park Bridge, on the chart the bridge is referred to as a swing bridge over Little Potato Slough Bridge.

I have since learned that it was a swing bridge when built in 1927. In 1991 it was rebuilt as something called a High Arch Bridge. I called Rio Vista Bridge and was routed to Tower Bridge in Sacramento. I gave Christopher at Tower Bridge my coordinates. Christopher said, "I have no idea where you are".

After awhile I figured it out: Delta waterways pass through a number of different counties, each with its own patchwork quilt of regulations and responsibilities. Most bridges span two counties, so it's a crapshoot to suggest that they are in one or another county.

For instance, the Orwood Railroad Bridge down near Discovery Bay is in San Joaquin County, the Walnut Grove Bridge is in Sacramento County, the bridge over Little Potato Slough is in San Joaquin County and the Rio Vista Bridge is in Solano County. Or some combination. Some of the bridges are operated by CalTrans while others are the responsibility of Homeland Security. It had been a long hot day and I found all this very confusing.

Finally, sitting in DM's cabin, I reached Greg @ at 7:30 pm. Greg is supervisor of District 10 of the California Department of Transportation. After we had worked out my location he asked me when I would like to pass under the bridge. We agreed upon 7 am and he assured me that he would personally make arrangements for it to open at 7 am the next morning.

Opening the Little Potato Slough Bridge

8.1.19 I woke at 5:30 am so I would have time for coffee. By 6:30 am Dura Mater's sails were raised and her Engine by Dave was idling. We circled around slowly and watched as five separate CalTrans trucks, an SUV and some kind of equipment truck with a ladder arrived at about 6:45. All the vehicles, filled with people, arrived from both sides of the slough and parked under the bridge.

Traffic stopped on Highway 12 and at precisely 7 am the bridge opened for Dura Mater and me. We skedaddled through to the other side of Little Potato Slough as fast as DM's little 11 hp engine could move. All the men waved to me as they stood beside their trucks drinking their coffee. Thank you, gentlemen. I appreciated your professional hospitality and the display of confidence.

Once Dura Mater and I had waved our way through the Little Potato Slough bridge, we sailed slowly over to where there are some really beautiful anchorages just the other side.

Anchorage north of Little Potato Slough Bridge

There was enough wind to for us to drift under sail, and although we could still hear the traffic on the highway, the little tule islands were green, still and quiet beneath us. We shared the water with only one fisherman, standing on a flat bottom boat, moving slowly along with a silent electric trolling motor.

DOWN THE SOUTH MOKELUMNE RIVER

It was too soon in the day to anchor, so after circling around and through the green grasses, Dura Mater and I returned to the bridge and turned to starboard. We were sailing due west and the wind was on the nose. The River is wide and we were sailing under blue skies. However, after 45 minutes of tacking, it was just too hot to keep doing that. On came the engine. This is one of the long stretches where the Army Corps of Engineers tore down most of the trees, so it's boring except for the birds.

If I were a bird aficionada I would probably have been ecstatic. There were thousands of birds along the way, and they seemed to be in charge of the landscape. No fewer than three huge, squawking blue herons flew above us, their mates in tall trees, one each at the top of a tree on its own tule island. Near one river marker there were hundreds of gees resting in place on what was obviously very shallow water. It wasn't too windy so I put up the beach umbrella and motored along toward Mount Diablo, which was in sight ahead of us the whole way.

After sailing west awhile we followed the South Mokelumne where it curves round at the fork and meets the North Mokelumne. That doesn't make much sense on paper, but it's true. Then it was time for breakfast. Over to starboard was Moore's Riverboat and I watched someone moving chairs around on the patio.

I sailed into a slip right in front of Moore's, jumped off to tie up and looked around to see if anyone was impressed by my docking prowess. That was when it became apparent no one was around and no one was impressed. Not even that waiter, who was staying inside where it was air conditioned. It also became obvious that no breakfast would be served here today. I was hungry and we were already here, so I stepped back aboard Dura Mater and made myself a pot of coffee. I put up my beach umbrella again, ate my granola in its shade, and drank the coffee

It got hotter, though, and once I had finished my breakfast I decided to head back to Owl Harbor. The mainsail was still up, so I shoved us off the dock. We headed back out through the cut in the tule grass toward the deeper channel which would have seemed reasonable except that, turns out, there's a big fat shoal right there and the depth is 4' at low tide. Dura Mater's draft is a whopping 4.5', so we got stuck hard in the mud right there.

I checked the chart: Four feet of water. I checked the tides on my handy app: below mean water level on this day. Imagine my relief to learn that my depth finder was very accurate. This was my third summer in the Delta and I had finally learned my lesson about thin water.

Dura Mater at Moore's Riverboat, Isleton

I tried to rock us out of the mud but that didn't work. I sat on the cabin top in the shade of the mainsail and watched as all the people in their sleek powerboats began to arrive for lunch. It seemed that every powerboat owner in the Delta came for lunch while we were stuck there in front of the restaurant. They avoided making eye contact, stopped laughing as they motored slowly by on their way to lunch. They acted like they were entering church, that's how embarrassed they were for us. I patted my boat, apologetic to have caused her to share my disgrace.

Oh well. These things happen. I finally gave in and called Vessel Assist.

Tommy and Michael of Vessel Assist

Good thing we have a Boat US subscription. Thank you to Phil Delano for the unlimited towing package that he donated to the winner of this year's Delta Doo Dah raffle: Me. And thank you to Tommy and Michael for arriving within ten minutes.

INTERVIEW WITH DEVERY STOCKON

8.2.19 When I first met Devery in 2017 I asked her whether I could interview her for this book. She said, "Sure", but she never seemed to find the time for me. In 2018 I asked again, but she declined. She was always busy, she said. This summer I walked up the levee road from my boat to the office, sauntered into the air conditioned community room and waited conspicuously. She knew I was there. The community room is a large, spacious room with comfortable chairs and big windows looking out on the alfalfa field. There are books and pods of Peets Coffee. I could have waited all day.

Devery finally joined me. Purposefully, which is how Devery does everything. She sat down and I handed her the microphone, which she pinned to her shirt.

Jackie: I wonder whether you could tell me about the first time you visited Owl Harbor?

Devery: *Sure. My husband and sister in law bought the marina. My husband thought it would be fun to own a marina. He doesn't work here. [Devery pauses and looks at me in a meaningful way). I was in between jobs and he asked me if I wanted to work at the marina. I asked, "What would I do?"*

He said, "Well, you would run it."

I said, "Maybe I should see it first."

He drove me up here. The minute we hit the entrance I just had this special feeling, this mental vision of what it could be. It hit me that this was a pretty special place.

We drove in and I fell in love with it. I was supposed to work part time, three days a week. I've never worked three days a week. I live and breathe here ... I love this marina. It had about twenty years of deferred maintenance. It was neglected. I was told by a number of people that boats came here to die and I said, "Not anymore."

We spent a couple of years just working to stop the hemorrhaging. The docks were in disrepair and everything here was gray ... but we just kinda kept going. [Devery laughs] *We had nowhere to go but up.*

We had a pretty colorful clientele at the time. I had to ask very few people to find a new home. A lot of them just left on their own, which was nice. We wished everybody the best. It wasn't going to be for everybody. We were changing things and, like most things that change: People don't like it.

This is our tenth year, our anniversary. In the beginning I remember thinking, "I can't wait to have a ten year anniversary celebration", and here we are! It kinda flew by.

Our original office and restrooms were two separate little buildings with really no foundation. Our office had a couple of desks and it leaned and it leaked from the time we bought the marina. The restrooms were next door. There was one shower and two heads in each of the restrooms. We figured at some point we would remodel the original office and restrooms.

I said, "We need just a little bit bigger office. Just a little bit bigger." It was really just a shoebox. When all the dogs and the cats would come in there wasn't really a lot of room for people. But they would come in, too. We had two chairs for people to sit down and the rest was standing room. It was funky.

That office was probably 400 square feet at the most. Now we have a 5000 square foot building. It houses our office with three desks and a beautiful counter, a kitchen and a clubhouse with a deck that goes all the way around. We have a huge deck out front and a barbeque so that people can relax and enjoy themselves. You get a beautiful breeze up there and there are lots of hummingbirds.

Downstairs of this two story building there are three big storage units. One of the storage units I've turned into a gym. We have a fitness room! A lot of people use that. They have a key for it so they can use it whenever they want, so it's better than 24 hour fitness.

The restrooms we changed from the one shower and two heads to three showers and four heads in each of the restrooms. I've always had a little fetish over nice bathrooms. Especially for the public, a bathroom that can be either bland and not real nice to go into. I spend so much time here I wanted to be sure that the restrooms are somewhere I enjoy going.

The fixtures and the photographs are those I've taken around the Delta. We have a large community garden and my co-workers have worked hard at that so I have some of their photographs in there of the flowers and plants. Then, of course, the wonderful Delta bridges are in the men's room. All the photographs in the men's rooms are black and white. They are heated restrooms, with teak furniture in the shower areas. We spent a year designing the building and then a year getting all the permits and building it. We've now been in this building for four years, in March of this year. It was 2016 when we finished it.

Where my husband and I live our house has lots of windows. One of the things that is important to us out here is being able to see everything. This is my first experience in the Delta: working here. I live in a beautiful place. It's absolutely incredible, the wildlife and the agriculture. You can see everything. Being on the water. Being able to see everything. We are an outdoor place.

We are the only business on Twitchell Island, which is wonderful. The rest is agriculture and they have turned some of the island into wetlands. Our property is twenty acres. Behind us are alfalfa fields. We have sandhill cranes. It's pretty exciting to see the wild life. We have owls here. We now have four owl houses that have occupancy pretty much year round on our property. We have owl season, turtle season, where the mother turtles come across from the water. They come over to our grass area.

She'll lay her eggs, cover them, and then she goes back to the water and never comes back. When the eggs hatch and the turtles cross back across the levee and go into the water. Turtle season is in May and June. How long the eggs take to hatch depends on the weather, usually about sixty days. We mark it on a calendar.

Javier, my co-worker, when he's mowing, he'll run into one of the moms and he'll watch. When he finds out where she's going he'll flag it so we know to keep an eye out and not mow over that area. Then we keep an eye on it. Javier and his family lived downstairs below the shower. Javier has been here for 26 years. My husband, Casey, says that Javier was the best thing about buying the marina.

When we had our old building we gathered some of those eggs and hatched our own baby turtle. We just waited. We had it inside in a pot. We had him as a pet for awhile and it was growing. We finally decided that he belonged back in nature so we released him back into the water. It was exciting.

With the windows, anybody who comes here, we want you to enjoy the outdoors. Like with people who go hunting or camping, they want to get back to nature. There are no big buildings here. There is no concrete. The building is made out of wood so that it is, hopefully, welcoming.

We have a lot of big pieces of wood, fir.

J: Could you tell me about the chickens?

D: *During maybe the second year we were here at the marina my co-worker, Curtis, built us a chicken coop and we bought 13 chickens, a baker's dozen. We thought they were all hens but you don't always know, and we ended up with two roosters. We had thirteen different kinds of chickens.*

One of the roosters was named Brutus, because even as a two day old chick "she" was mean, she was pushy with the others. After about a year Brutus took the lead and after about a year he decided he didn't really like me so he decided he would come after me. I would go in and gather eggs. We give away all the eggs to all our tenants and guests, we like to share them.

I walked in with a stick just to keep her off me and finally I got sick and tired of it and so I told Curtis, "we need to do something about Brutus, this isn't working." The roosters wouldn't let me in to feed the hens. So the next day we had barbeque. We ate the two roosters. Javier's wife made a mole sauce and we had chicken mole. Seven men and I ate the giant rooster. It's hard but it's also part of nature and part of the process. We don't make a habit of eating our chickens.

We have two big coops but as they get older they slow down and we have a reputation to keep our tenants set with eggs. So when they get to be about three years old I bring in about fifteen new chicks. We raise them in the office until they're old enough to go downstairs, then we put them in a playpen area downstairs, then when they get big enough and it's warm enough we move them into their own coop. So everything kind of rotates.

J: It sounds like crop rotation. Chicken rotation. Did you study it? Read about how to do it?

D: *No, I just make it up. I've been watching them for 10 years. At least every day I spend time with them. I can see how they react to each other. Once a chicken becomes ill the other chickens peck at it and they will go until it's dead. And chickens are carnivorous. They're pretty violent. We don't eat them if they die. Chickens are really only good to eat if they're under three years old.*

At one point we had a chicken named Queenie. She was a beautiful chicken and she was getting henpecked. I wanted to save her cuz she was one of my favorites, so I bought her a little coop and we refer to that as the infirmary.

J: Is that Queenie in there now?

D: *No. That's Vivian. Vivian is a rooster. Vivian was in with two other roosters and Vivian was the top rooster. I don't know what happened, but I went down there one day and the other roosters had made Vivian mad and Vivian just continued to go after these other two roosters. Unfortunately for Vivian, he was not the bigger rooster, he was smaller than the other two so they wouldn't go after her, but when I went into the coop with Vivian she would try to circumvent me and go after them. So I picked her up and said, "Vivian, I adore you, but you're just going to have to go into the infirmary."*

Devery Stockon, weed killer

She's been in there for a month and a half. And she hurt her leg because when she shakes her head sometimes she'll fall over. I just want to make sure she's strong enough to go back into the coop.

Every year we move the coops. We rotate the chicken coops because that fertilizes the ground. Our goal is to have a watering system because we just don't have the time to hand water everything. It's very time consuming. There is a lot of property. It takes five days to mow and weed-eat the property.

Javier Lopez has been here for 26 years. He and his wife and their youngest son have lived here the whole time. They used to live below our old building. He and his son and his wife now live in their own house on the property. His oldest son, Luis, is a co-worker and has lived here for 22 years. He's married and lives in Oakley with two little boys.

Javier is an avid fisherman. He has four boats. His daughter has four kids, including identical twin girls. And two boys. They spend a lot of time here on the weekends with grandma and grandpa. To me this has always been an ideal place for families as well as pets because it's safe and you're outside.

In our building we have a really large flatscreen tv which is just for the Superbowl, the World Series, something like that. We have overnight guests with kids who arrive and they ask, can the kids watch a movie? And I say, no, I'm sorry, they need to be outside. You can watch a movie at home. You don't get the outside and the wildlife and the fresh air ... you don't get that at home.

J: And you have lots and lots of books.
D: We found out early on that boaters are readers.

J: Behind this building are fields of alfalfa?
D: Yes, Alfalfa. Most of Twitchell Island is owned by the state government and leased to farmers. On Andrews Island, just across the road, there is corn. Owl Harbor has been here since 1966. It started out as just a few docks.

J: You bought Owl Harbor as an investment?

D: *If you can call a marina an investment.* (laughs) *It's like a boat! They're not investments. It's a labor of love.*

Devery, with her mother and the Owl Harbor kids

You know what it is, Jackie? It's a lifestyle. And it's the quality of life that you want to have. I just want to have a nice place where people like to go that's still in the funky delta. I think that's what it's about.

It's not about making money. It's about how you spend your life and what brings you joy. For me, being here with my co-workers? And my family and friends? A lot of the people who live here are my friends. It's a family. Owl Harbor is a community.

Owl Harbor was my Delta base four summers running. While I was there I watched Devery work her magic with tenants and visitors. She ran out to flag drivers down if they went too fast up the levee road, herded grown-ups as they participated in floatie races on the water and donned a hazmat suit before riding out to attack the weeds. Devery is a force of nature.

GEORGIANA SLOUGH

8.10.19 After the Meet and Greet with Vessel Assist I'm determined to be a more careful sailor. Before I sail now I look at the tide book as part of my planning for the next day before I go to sleep. According to the local tide app I should be good to go at 10 am tomorrow. So I sleep the REM rest of the well-organized sailor.

If you wake up on your boat and it's already hot, that means you've slept in. After two orange yolky eggs from Owl Harbor chickens, lots of strong coffee and, a quick dip into the water off Dura Mater's stern, I raise the sails and we're off down Seven Mile Slough to locate and sail up the famous Georgiana Slough. Just so we can say we did it.

It seems as though everybody who has ever been to the Delta on a boat of any kind talks about Georgiana Slough. They say things like,

> "Georgiana Slough is so beautiful! We *love* Georgiana Slough!" or

"Have you been to Georgiana Slough yet? *We've* been to Georgiana Slough!" or

"You've *got* to go up Georgiana Slough! You'll *love* Georgiana!"

Contrary person, singlehanded sailor that I am, all the hype was enough to put me off Georgiana Slough. However, this is my third summer in the Delta and I want to go to Walnut Grove. So off we go, up Georgiana Slough, Dura Mater and I. We will find out for ourselves how nice it is, thank you very much.

Exiting Seven Mile Slough into the San Joaquin, at least fifty zippy cigarette boats passed us heading down river. At least fifty. Big engines, beautiful sparkly paint jobs with flames along their hulls, and filled with people. They left surprisingly small wakes for such fast boats. Dura Mater was the only sailboat on the water.

We turned to port at the Delta loop and passed Pirates Lair. Circled around and gave Moore's Riverboat a WIDE berth. DM and I weren't falling for that old trick again. I have decided to discipline myself and limit the use of my "unlimited towing package" from Vessel Assist. I don't want the fellas start to call me by name over the radio. I can hear them now:

"Hi, Jackie! Where are you stuck in the mud today?" That would be so embarrassing.

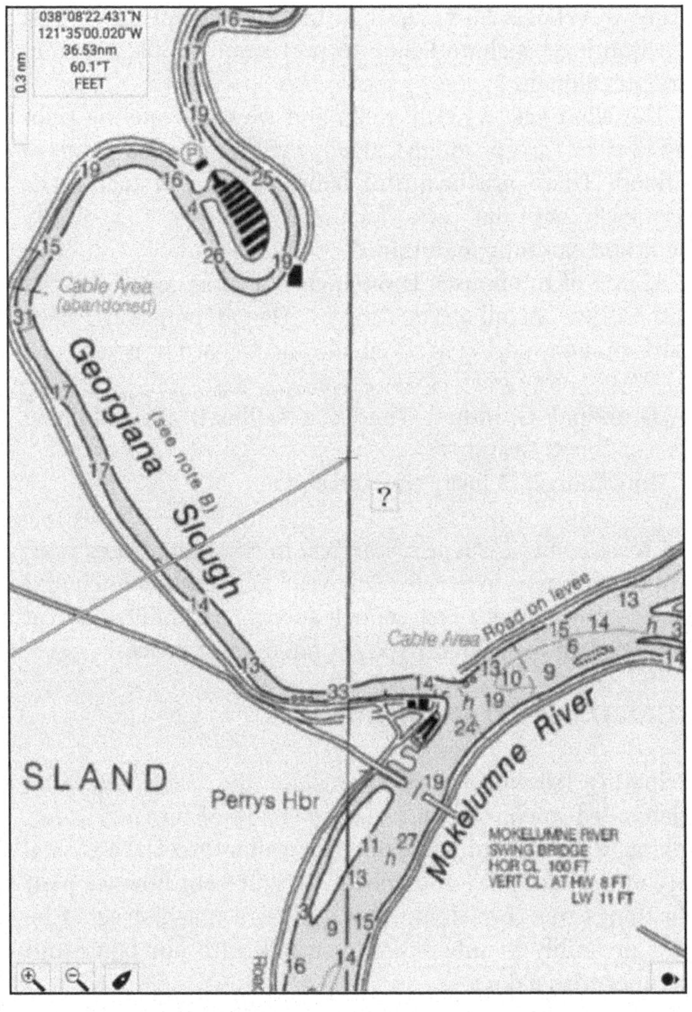

We reached the Mokelumne Bridge at 11:40 am and I called Demi Stewart for an opening on VHF Channel 9.
I asked about Janet Wilcox, but Demi said Janet isn't in charge of the Mokelumne Bridge anymore.

I was reminded of how polite are the bridge operators. Although Janet Wilcox told me the term is not bridge tenders, they are all awfully nice when you ask politely.

I was going to stop at B&W resort so I could twirl around on the counter stool and eat a softie. But the fuel dock was full of little powerboats filling up their tanks, so I kept going, past the swimming beach and then to port again. Voila! I was in Georgiana Slough!

The wind was wsw 14 knots and we were moving right along upriver (or up slough), slowly drifting in what is left of the flood. There are beautiful houses there, all facing the water, each with its own dock. Nice houses, too. Pretty designs and carefully maintained.

At one of the houses I watched as a little boy registered that there was a sailboat drifting by. He ran across the deck toward someone sitting in the shade and I heard him yell,

"Grandpa! Grandpa! There's a sailboat! How do you drive a sailboat, Grandpa?"

How, indeed? I just point and shoot.

I have come to savor my arrival in the Delta every year, so am in no hurry to arrive. This year I've already anchored for the first time, with just enough success and failure to feel experienced and confident. Too confident, as it proves.

SINGLE HANDED ANCHORING

Anticipating trouble ahead, I consider the issue regarding singlehanded anchoring in a narrow body of moving water. Thinking is where the singlehanded sailor excels. We have plenty of time to talk to ourselves, to figure out how we plan to do things our own damned way. We're not distracted by friends or family members. We also talk with our boats and sometimes with a dog.

Now, the party line regarding anchoring in the Delta (among sailors with crew) is to drop either a stern or bow anchor, then tie the line at the other end of your boat to a tree branch on shore. Obviously it's easier to anchor that way when you have at least two people on your sailboat, because then you have at least one person to yell at while you do it. The idea is that you as the skipper can tell your crew to get into the dinghy, kayak, inflatable raft, paddle board, whatever, and make his/her way to shore where he/she is expected to tie a stern line to a branch, tree root, anything else.

As far as I can tell, this requires the crew member to become wet, muddy, sweaty and upset. Sometimes the inflatable becomes punctured, sometimes the kayak or paddle board tips over, and then the yelling really starts. Well, now, how is a singlehander supposed to accomplish anchoring without all that drama? I don't have a kayak or an inflatable anything, and I don't want to have to buy one just for Georgiana Slough. I don't have crew to order around, either. However, I've got this perfectly nice sailboat. In other words, I plan to anchor without someone else to boss around.

Here is a thought I will share. Just another small but crucial detail that a singlehander needs to remember: it is very important to make sure everything is in place ahead of time. Like raising a spinnaker solo: think things through, double check to make sure lines will run free; trust your autopilot, then move fast!

1. Don't anchor in water depth where the weeds can still grow. If you are sailing offshore this means where the kelp are no longer able to grow. In the Delta weeds grow where the sun is still able to reach them. I have been told to not anchor in less than 15' but I think deeper is probably better.

2. Don't use the whole length of your rode, especially if you are anchoring bow and stern. You'll need to pay out more line according to whether you start at one end or the other, then you'll want to snug up. You never want to use all your line. Never. Never. Never.

3. And finally, it's always a good idea to confirm there are no twigs or grass in the propeller before starting the engine every morning. And if there is? Well, you climb down the ladder on your transom to dig them out. A ladder is a necessary piece of equipment in the Delta.

GETTING STUCK IN THE MUD

While we are being metaphysical, I will digress and offer my opinion that getting stuck in the mud in a keel boat is a wonderful adventure. I recommend it. But it's best experienced unexpectedly, because then it's an opportunity for a story. If you plan ahead to get stuck in the mud it just doesn't have the same effect. When you find yourself stuck (and unable to get unstuck, that's the key), you are sometimes reminded of words you might think you've forgotten. And sailors know lots of words. You might already know this.

Some stories about being stuck in the mud are real stories based upon fact. Some stories become embellished over time, which usually makes them even better stories. Some of them are big fat lies, and those are the ones most difficult to characterize. Is this person a really good story teller? A particularly gifted embellisher? Or a big fat fibber? I leave you to discern.

It can be scary to get stuck in the mud, especially when the wind is howling and you were not expecting an adventure and your anchor is not ready to deploy: Meaning your anchor is somewhere in the very bottom of your lazarette under the coils of old rotting rope and recovered fenders. That is scary, but you've dealt with more difficult issues in your lifetime, so you just dive down in there and grab it up.

Don't let the lazarette fall down on your head when you do that, and DO NOT, I REPEAT, DO NOT go so far down into the lazarette so that it locks closed behind you. That happened to a former Commodore of the Singlehanded Sailing Society, Bill Merrick, on his way across the Pacific to Kauai. An ex-Marine, Bill didn't stay trapped for very long.

Dura Mater is a heavy displacement boat and I use a large aluminum plow anchor that a friend gave me before he sailed off into the sunset. In the beginning I used it because I wanted to make sure that we didn't go off hook while I slept. However, I have come to believe that my little Danforth is adequate for most anchoring in the Delta.

MOKELUMNE RIVER TO OXBOW MARINA

We reached Oxbow Marina @ 12:45, tied up to the fuel dock where the depth was 19'6" and filled the tank with diesel. There is also gas available. I went inside the office and bought an ice cream cone, then we were off, on our way to Walnut Grove.

From Oxbow Marina we continue up Georgiana with a gentle breeze behind us, just enough to drift along under sail. Georgiana Slough winds around and around. It is delightful, except that DM's mainsail has a big leech, which keeps catching on the backstay. So I lower sail down to that first reefing point, the one that's useless in the big wind of the San Francisco Bay. It is not a deep enough reefing point for a windy day, but perfect for today because it balloons out and catches every bit of wind that's out there.

Lots of gybing today. Back and forth. Back and forth. Georgiana has lots of curves, and we go 'round all of 'em. It is a particularly hot day. Of course it's hot. It's August and we're in the Delta.

I am determined to anchor somewhere along Georgiana Slough for the night. Trouble is, Georgiana is surrounded by trees just waiting to grab my boat. Once we have gone under Tyler Island Bridge I start considering the merits of potential anchorages.

I look and I look for a place to drop the bow anchor, but those trees are everywhere! What I need is a nice little muddy beach with no trees above. Finally I find what looks like the perfect place to drop anchor and spend the night. It is about time, too, because I am really sweaty and tired.

We motor slowly past a big, crooked, half submerged tree root to port, just past overhanging trees. It is a spot with big tall shrubs, but no trees. Motoring past the shrubs growing at the shore's edge, I put the engine into neutral, then go forward to crouch at DM's bow. I drop anchor and let out rode as we drift slowly backward in the ebb. Drifting,

drifting, drifting, getting closer to that tree branch, which I lasso with my stern line. Gotcha! I feel so successful!

Okay. So far, so good. Go quickly forward again, snug up the bow line, right? Then back to snug up the stern line, in order to pull Dura Mater in out of the thru-way. Now, though, the ebb is increasing, which pulls her bow out too far, so I snug up the bow line again. Back and forth. Back and forth. That brings us closer and closer to those tall shrubs.

They reach out and grab Dura Mater's portside shrouds. Oh no! Oh no! I rush up to the bow. In order to get up there I have to shove through the branches and dried blackberry bushes that are filling up my cockpit and getting stuck between the cabin top and lifelines.

A big blackberry branch catches my leg and I can feel it tear the skin on my calf. I leap forward and pull up the bow anchor, which causes Dura Mater to swing further round, to starboard all the way, deeper now into still taller shrubs. Then we are into the trees, anchored now by her stern line, and still tied to that damned rotten tree root.

Concerned now about tree parts getting stuck in the prop, I reach down through the foliage in the cockpit and turn off the engine. There we are, facing downstream in the ebb, when a towering pile of dry branches showers down on me, full of whole sheets of spider webs and whole families of spiders. I feel them crawling around on my legs and arms and then something falls on my head. Nothing heavy, but SOMETHING CREEPY! So I kind of panic and start doing a little Indian dance, head down, whimpering. I am cursing and sweating, trying to shake creepy crawlies out of my hair.

That's when I hear it: The call of that rare Delta specimen: Richard the Kayaker.

"Hi."

I look down from DM's port gunwhale, and there he is, floating just below me on the water, smiling up as he effortlessly maintains position with deft handling of his paddle. He doesn't ask if I need help. Oh no. Delta people are very polite that way. They don't want to embarrass anyone. Call it the Delta style.

Richard the Kayaker

"Oh. Hello." I say. I try insouciance.

"Beautiful day, isn't it?" He pretends not to notice that my rigging is full of branches, there is blood dripping down my leg and my hair is full of leaves and spider webs.

"Although it's hot. Hotter than yesterday," he says.

"Hmmmm," say I. Twitching.

I start tossing branches and twigs out of the cockpit, like it is ordinary housekeeping. With the ineffable graciousness that is the hallmark of people who live in the Delta, this smiling man in his kayak acts as if we are meeting up at the grocery. Ignoring my obvious and wild eyed stupidity, he calmly compliments me.

"You have a beautiful boat," he says, which is a line meant to calm the most savage of beasts, and maybe to give me still more moments to collect myself. His composure is soothing. Like a doctor after successful surgery.

Then we had a nice conversation, Richard in his kayak, me in Dura Mater's cockpit. Turns out, Richard has a ski boat and he was thinking of taking it down to the Bay Area: What did I think about that? Well, I said, I didn't see many ski boats in the Bay Area, but maybe he could come down in the winter.

And ski real early in the morning. Somewhere. He nodded thoughtfully and pretended to consider his options, but really? He was just giving me time to wind down.

Richard looked off into the distance politely, while I scratched my leg and threw more dried branches and spider webs into the water. We watched together as everything floated downstream.

"Hey!" Richard gestured toward the rotten log branch as if he had forgotten it was there. "Were you thinking of anchoring here?"

Why yes, I admitted that I had indeed thought of anchoring here. But I had changed my mind. I no longer wanted to anchor in this particular location. He nodded thoughtfully.

"I live just up there." He pointed upstream. "Sailboats usually don't anchor here. There's an anchorage just ahead, around the curve. I usually see them up there."

"Hmmmm," said I. "Well, maybe I'll have to try that anchorage next time."

Richard indicated the stern line, firmly attached to the submerged tree root, twenty feet away. So near yet so far away.

"Would you like me to help you with that line?" The way he said it? I would be doing him a favor, he was that sweet.

"Thank you," I said. "I would be grateful to you."

With a flick of his wrist, Richard freed Dura Mater and me from the stern line that bound us to Georgiana Slough. I turned on my Engine by Dave and we started slowly upstream. Richard paddled alongside for awhile. He promised to look me up before he brings his ski boat to the Bay and I gave him my boat card. But I haven't heard from him yet. If anybody out there is acquainted with Richard the kayaker from Georgiana Slough, please let me know. I'd love to take him out to lunch, or breakfast, or dinner and try to return the favor of his generosity in August 2019.

I was discarding small tree branches and leaves all the way from Georgiana Slough to Walnut Grove, which was just

Tyler Island Bridge

ahead past two more bridges and through several more turns in the Slough. Then we were under the Georgiana Bridge and there was the Walnut Grove Bridge looming over us on the Old Sacramento.

WALNUT GROVE

8.10.19 Dura Mater and I were finally in Walnut Grove. We passed under three bridges today: the Mokelumne, where Demi Stewart is the operator, the Tyler Island Bridge (Tyler Island is to starboard all along the Georgiana), and finally, the Georgiana Slough Bridge, which is located just south of where Georgiana empties into the Old Sacramento River at Walnut Grove.

I forgot that the anchor was still hanging from Dura Mater's bow, and we landed with a big THUMP at Dagmar's Landing. We were directly across the river from both the public pier and with steps further down, what is known as the fishing pier. Dagmar's Landing is just below the Levee Road from the Central Market.

When I stepped off DM and examined my danforth at her bow I saw that it was full of quagga mussels, some of them the size of dimes, some the size of quarters. Wait a minute. Don't I pay an extra registration fee to keep quaggas out of fresh water? Or is it the other way around? There are so many mysteries in the Delta

Central Market Walnut Grove

It's a beautiful, cool Saturday night. I leave Dura Mater to walk across Walnut Grove Bridge to the The Pizza Factory which is busy with a line of customers. I order a small pizza with mushrooms, onions and spinach and sit in the window where I can watch everyone while I drink still more tall glasses of water.

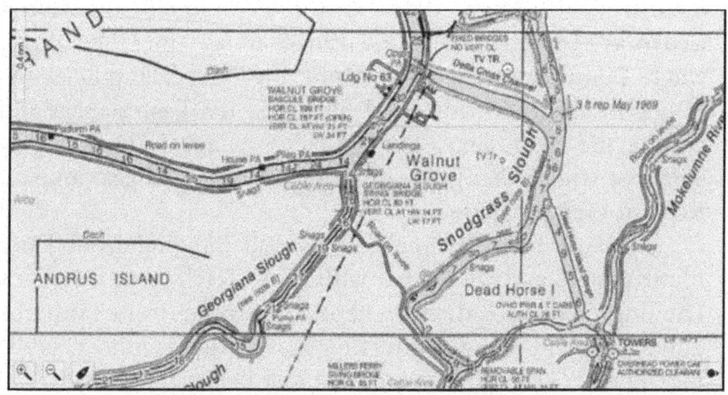

What did I see at The Pizza Factory? A little boy with Down syndrome, about 8 years old, who watched his dad intently as he gave the young woman their order. When his father leaned on the counter, the little boy leaned on the counter. He looked down to see how his father crossed his left leg over his ankle and slowly, deliberately crossed his own left leg just the same way. Careful imitation is the way boys learn from their fathers everywhere.

8.11.19 I woke up early Sunday morning and walked across the Walnut Grove bridge to Alma's River Café. It opened at 7:00 am and I was first one in the door. For a brief time I was the only customer, and I was able to sit at the counter and chat with Mr. Phat (pronounced Pat) while Mrs. Phat cooked me bacon, eggs and toast.

Peter and Vanna Phat, owners of Alma's Café

Peter and Vanna Phat bought Alma's Café from a family friend. The Phats are from Cambodia. They have two children, little girls aged 3 months and 8 years, and Mrs.

Phat's mother cares for them while she and her husband run the restaurant here in Walnut Grove. They have lived in Pittsburgh for 12 years and plan to expand hours in order to serve dinner as soon as more relatives arrive to help.

Sunday breakfast at Alma's Café

I talked with Mr. Phat about how different are the breakfasts eaten by Delta farmers and those eaten by Cambodian farmers. Mr. Phat raised his eyebrows and nodded his head. He told me that farmers eat much larger breakfasts here in Walnut Grove. Typically Cambodians eat a type of porridge made from rice with maybe a bit of dried fish, or maybe just a croissant and coffee.

Here in Walnut Grove Mr. and Mrs. Phat have had to learn how to make hash browns. My own breakfast arrived as the door opened to more customers and Mr. Phat became too busy to talk. The coffee was strong and the food delicious.

INTERVIEW WITH JAMES WHITAKER

8.11.19 After breakfast at Alma's, I called the Walnut Grove bridge operator and asked if I could come up to interview him.

Mr. James Whitaker said, "Sure", so I walked across the bridge and knocked on the door. It's a side door with no sign on the outside. He opened the door and before he invited me in he asked:

"Now, do I get an autographed copy of this book?"
"You certainly do," I replied.

We exchanged business and boat cards and then he stepped aside. There I was, in my second bridge office. I handed him the microphone, he clipped it to his collar, and this is what Mr. Whitaker had to say:

Jackie: Last year I interviewed Janet Wilcox, and she explained that I can't take a photograph of you in here. This bridge is under Homeland Security and we don't want the Russians to know about all those red and green buttons. So I'm not going to ask to photograph you. I do have a really nice photograph of the man at Tyler Island Bridge, though. He came out and waved to me.

James: *Oh, that would be Lee. He's a good guy.*

Jackie: How did you come to be a bridge operator?

JW: *Max Tobias was a bridge operator and he was my book keeper. I had a business going there, I was a general contractor. I did a lot of boating on the Delta. I talked to him and I said, 'I'd like to come up, work those bridges, just one day, see how ..."*

Time went by, and he called me to ask, "Were you serious about that?" I said, "Yes I was". He said, "They need somebody. I mentioned you and they want you to come in and interview." So I went in for the interview and I must've impressed them because they were eager to hire me.

J: What year was that?

JW: *I think 1999. 98 or 99. I told them 'I've got a business. I just want to do this for a short period of time. Maybe one or two days a week. They said, 'that's fine. That's just great.' So I came to work and I was working 6, 7 days in a row. I told them, 'I can't do this. I've got a business.' They called me in, we sat down, and they said, "What if we offered you a permanent position?" I thought about that. I said, "yeah, I would like that. I've got to shut my business down slowly and so forth." So. Here I am, twenty something years later.*

J: When they called you in, they must have known you were a responsible person, that you lived in the Delta. What part of that, do you think, persuaded them that you were the person to hire? Because I know that they're not going to take just anybody.

JW: *Well, this is a pretty simple job. It was my experience, I think, I worked for Skyline Mobile homes for twelve years. I was production manager. I had that experience. I drove a lot of machinery. The DOT is what handles the bridges so they've got equipment, they were thinking, 'Okay, [he] could go to other departments in the DOT (Department of Transportation) if it came to that.'*

J: Have you ever been called to operate other equipment?

JW: *No.*

J: Janet told me that you're not called a bridge tender, you're called a bridge operator.

JW: *Yeah, Some people, they don't like being called a bridge tender. I don't know why. I don't know what it is. Most women, you call 'em a bridge tender, they get upset and say: 'I'm a bridge operator. I'm not a bridge tender.'* [James shrugs, sits back in his chair].

J: I was just up in Lodi at Tower Park. That's in San Joaquin County. I sailed up there and there was a lot of confusion with regard to me being able to reach the bridge operator.

JW: *That bridge doesn't open very much. So about once a month or once every other month they come down and do a test opening. When you requested an opening, they probably said, 'okay, this is a good time to do our test opening.'* [laughs]

Walnut Grove Bridge in the Deadman Position

Here at Walnut Grove we have a great maintenance crew. They come down once a month. They lube it, they go underneath, check it. They open the bridge. They check everything. They keep the bridges running. We have very little problems with our bridges.

J: Do they do a different bridge every month?
JW: *Yes. Sacramento has four bridges: two on the Sacramento River and two on Georgiana Slough. The Tyler Island Bridge, Georgiana Slough, Walnut Grove and Freeport. They usually come on the first of the month. Within that first week. They spend a day on each one.*

J: I talked to somebody this morning at breakfast in Alma's restaurant. He said that in the summertime sometimes the bridge can buckle? They close the bridge? Is that true? It's such a powerful bridge. How can that happen?
JW: *This bridge here? It's a bascule bridge. When it gets above 100 degrees the bridge deck gets hot and it stretches and when it comes down it overlaps and you can't have cars going across.*

So what we do, we put a sprinkler system on the bridge so when it reaches 95 [degrees] you have to close the bridge to traffic, turn the sprinklers on and run 'em for awhile, try to keep the bridge cool. It depends. What I do, I open it all the way up, specially if you got a breeze, stand it straight up for about ten minutes and the wind blowing through it, and the weight of the bridge will cause it to settle.

We are interrupted by what sounds like the loud ringing of a phone.

James: *Okay, we're going to open the bridge! We've got a pedestrian here, gotta get her across. Most of them run .... C'mon, I'll show you how we do this ... first off, turn the key on. You hear the bells ringing?*

J: I do. And you come out of this office physically to make sure it's working?

JW: *Yeah. We've got the pin out there in the center, we've got pins out there in the center. We pull the pin back so the bridge can go up. Then the red light comes on... We put it on the raised position, called the dead man.*

We both watched as the bridge slowly rose over the river.
J: It's beautiful! What a feat of engineering!
JW: *You look at this bridge. It was built in, I think, '55. All the moving parts ... It'll go straight up. The barges come through, with big cranes....*

There are lots of different kinds of loud bells and warning sounds that continue. James and I are both laughing, enjoying the cacophony of sound. When the bridge has been lowered again we stay outside the office, watching the cars pass over the bridge in front of us.

James Whitaker, Walnut Grove Bridge operator

J: What kind of a boat do you have?
JW: *Right now I've got a 24' Bayliner Trophy for fishing.*

J: I noticed those people who just came through the bridge, they were trolling. The sunlight hit the fishing wires and one was lime green, one was orange and one was pink. They were beautiful!
JW: *Fluorescent line.*

J: Are they like marine wiring, the different colors are different sized diameter?
JW: *I believe so. I never use it.*

J: What do you fish for?
JW: *Mainly striped bass. The biggest one I ever caught was 24 lbs but they've been up over 40 lbs.*

J: What's your average catch?
JW: *Probably about 12 lb. Sometimes you can go out there and you catch a lot of 'em, sometimes you don't catch any. The last couple of years it's been bad fishing here. It's been slow. The stripers, they come up at different times. You have your spring run, your summer run, your fall run.*

The tide has a lot to do with fishing. It's just a hobby with me. I like going out and fishing. I can go out and drop a hook, put the line in the water, sit there and have a good time. Your bass fishermen, they're serious fishermen. They spend thousands of dollars on rod, it has to be just right. The line has to be just so right and the knot has to be tied just right. I'm not a serious fisherman.

J: Who cleans your fish?
JW: *I do.*

J: This is the public dock [I gesture] and then this is the fishing dock. People were already here early this morning. They had chairs and coolers and they were already fishing at 6:30.
JW: *When the salmon run that dock over there is just shoulder to shoulder with people. In the spring the salmon come up ... they hit the ocean around the first of the year,*

they usually come up here around May and June. They'll go all the way up to the mountains, into those streams up there, and lay their eggs.

I used do boating down in Southern California. Mainly in the Salton Sea. We'd go to Lake Havasu once in awhile. Then when I moved up here I started boating, bought a bigger boat and it's different. And the sailboats: I had trouble with the sailboats. You're going down the river and all of a sudden this sailboat, he's here and he's crossing your bow because he's tacking, you know? I'm sitting there, wondering, 'what's wrong with that guy?' You know? So, you've gotta learn: That's how he moves. I guess if he's going against the wind.

So, okay, you watch a little closer. It's fun. You got a lot of different boats. I go down to the Bay every once in awhile and you got the big freighters and you got the tugs and the ferries. [he laughs] *The ferry boats, they don't seem like they give way to anybody. 'Hey! I'm coming through! You stop, get out of the way, I'll run over you'* [we're both laughing].
I love the Bay.

J: What is your boat called? Is it a cabin cruiser?
JW: *Well, yeah. I've got a little cabin on it, but it's just for fishing. It's a Trophy Troll, built for rough water and ocean. Alaska.*

J: How is the shape of the hull built for the ocean?
JW: *It's a v hull.*

J: Where do you go, when you go to the Bay?
JW: *We usually go to Pier 40 or Pier 39. Sausalito. I used to have a buddy, that's where he fished. Sausalito. I'd go down there. Usually around June. July.*

J: That's when it's windy! When you go out in your boat, you're okay in that chop?
JW: *Oh, yeah. That Trophy. That's what it was built for – the Potato Patch area.*

J: You go out in the ocean?
JW: *Oh, yeah. If you're going out underneath the Gate, over to the right there's a little bay over there, they do a lot of rock fishing over there. So you'll see a lot of boats just drifting out there. We go up to Duxbury when the salmon are running.*

J: You must have a big engine.
JW: *Well, yeah. It's an inboard. It's a 350 cu inch. It's probably about a hundred something horses. It's like a car engine, you know.*

J: One year I sailed back from Drakes Bay and there were some serious fishing boats at Duxbury Reef! With the big spotlights on at night. And the huge long arms!
JW: *Yeah, those are your professional fishermen. They've got maybe twenty, thirty lines out. Those guys, they're out there 24 hours a day. They don't sleep.*

J: So you catch salmon out there in the ocean and people catch 'em up here. What's the difference? Are they fatter here or in the ocean?
JW: *Much better in salt water. Once they enter fresh water, that's when they start changing. Salmon are a beautiful fish. If you catch 'em in the ocean they're beautiful, but when they start up out of the salt water they get real soft and their nose starts to grow and it curls up and they've got teeth that come out.*

> *When they get upstream to spawn they all die. You look at the run, especially in Alaska, salmon, what they go through – they've got the professional fishermen out there throwing their nets, catching 'em. Then you have your weekend fishermen out there catching 'em.*

Once they enter the fresh water and they start up river, everybody's fishing here. They've got lines out. The salmon will go a hundred miles and then the bears are out there catching them and the birds are eating. It's amazing that we still have salmon. It's an ordeal just to get up there to spawn.

James and I ponder the fate of the salmon for a few minutes, watching as small pleasure boats full of people head up the Sacramento River beneath us.

J: Do you have a sailboat story for me?
JW: *I was working Freeport Bridge and a sailboat was coming down river. He called for an opening. It takes you a little while sometimes. You've gotta clear the bridge, get the cars all off. He was ... well, I shouldn't say anything ... Anyway, as I was starting to open the bridge I told him, "Skipper, you've gotta back off." You know? "The bridge doesn't open real fast."*

He says, "Okay, I've got it!" But his timing was off. The Mast caught on the bridge. The river was running strong and he went down and the boat did this, but then it broke loose and he popped back up. So he goes underneath the bridge and he calls me on the radio and says, "My timing was off." I said, "Yeah, it sure was!" He asked, "Did I do any damage to the bridge?"

I said, "I don't know. I'm gonna have to check that out. I've got your boat name and CF # so you might be hearing from us. [James laughs, shaking his head]. *So he went home down river. There was no damage.*

Between Memorial Day to the September Jazz Festival in Sacramento? I've seen Tyler Bridge have over 250 openings on that weekend. That's how many people were going up to Sacramento. And those openings were from people who needed the bridge to open for them. That doesn't include smaller boats[that didn't require the bridge to open.

Big boats, too. The yacht clubs would go up. I was at Tower Park Yacht Club and we'd get invited up there every year. Sacramento Yacht Club would invite us up. This bridge here? We'd probably have to open the bridge here a hundred times over that weekend. And we're tall compared to Tyler. This year, Memorial Day, I think four boats went up. Mainly motorboats. We don't get a lot of sailboats up here. I think most of the sailboats will go up Steamboat for some reason. Less bridges. If you got a bunch of sailboats coming up, then everybody wants the bridge open. You try to get 'em to bunch up because you've got traffic to worry about. You know?

James gives a big sigh and looks at me meaningfully.
He says, "*Sailboaters. They're a little **different**.*"

J: They won't bunch up, is that it?
JW: *They don't like it. Because some of 'em are faster than others and ... They say, "I'm not gonna wait for them! Open the bridge for me!"*

And another thing about sailboating. I don't know about yours. Most of 'em – a lot of 'em – don't have radios! Or they can't get to the radio. I don't know what the deal is, they're settin back there and they have these little canned horns, you know? I'm sitting in here and ... [he gestures around the sound-proof room and shrugs] I don't hear that little air horn going off, you know [we both laugh]?

So they get upset and they end up calling Rio Vista by cell phone and complain: "I've been circling here for twenty minutes!"

I say, "Well, I'm sorry! I didn't hear you. Where's your radio?" [James shakes his head mournfully] *That's one of the little deals with sailboaters. They've probably got it inside the cabin. Do you have a handheld? Most of 'em don't.*

J: Of course I have a handheld. How often does that happen? The sailors I know understand basic radio protocol. It's a safety issue, too.

James shakes his head again, smiling patiently. The last thing James Whitaker tells me is this:

"Sailboating. It seems like a lot of work to me."

I thank him for his time and carefully write down his contact information. We part friends, even though he knows that I am an unrepentant sailboater.

Walnut Grove to Steamboat Slough = 5.85 nm, average 3.5 knots under engine, 1 hour, 40 minutes.

8.11.19 Leaving Walnut Grove @ 2:47 pm, Dura Mater and I started optimistically up the river under sail.
After the first turn to port, though, the wind was straight on the nose and the river stretched into the distance. So, on came the Engine by Dave and we motorsailed slowly all the way up to Steamboat Slough. I was ever hopeful for a shift in the wind so I could sail again, but was disappointed the whole way.

The old Sacramento River is a wide flat stretch of water once you get past Walnut Grove today, and there is blue sky and river as far as I can see. There are lots of families in power boats pulling skiers or kids in inner tubes.

It is Sunday, and there are lots of SeaDoo riders racing up and down the water, and large cabin cruisers full of groups of people. I noticed huge itinerant snags along the way, too. Although it is wide and deep, I don't think I would want to motor fast up the Sacramento in the dark.

Steamboat Slough Bridge is to port at what is known as Steamboat Landing. Approximately one nm down from the Steamboat Slough Bridge is an anchorage opposite a house that resembles a ski chalet. The current is very strong here at the confluence of the slough and the river.

Steve Cameron told me that I could only find tide and current books at bait shops in the Delta, not from Marina offices. I know this is true because when I asked for such a book at the Pittsburg Marina the harbormaster had no idea what I was talking about. He gave me a current book for the GG Bridge. Then he waved his hand as if to shoo away a bug, which is the Delta version of rolling one's eyes, only slightly more polite.

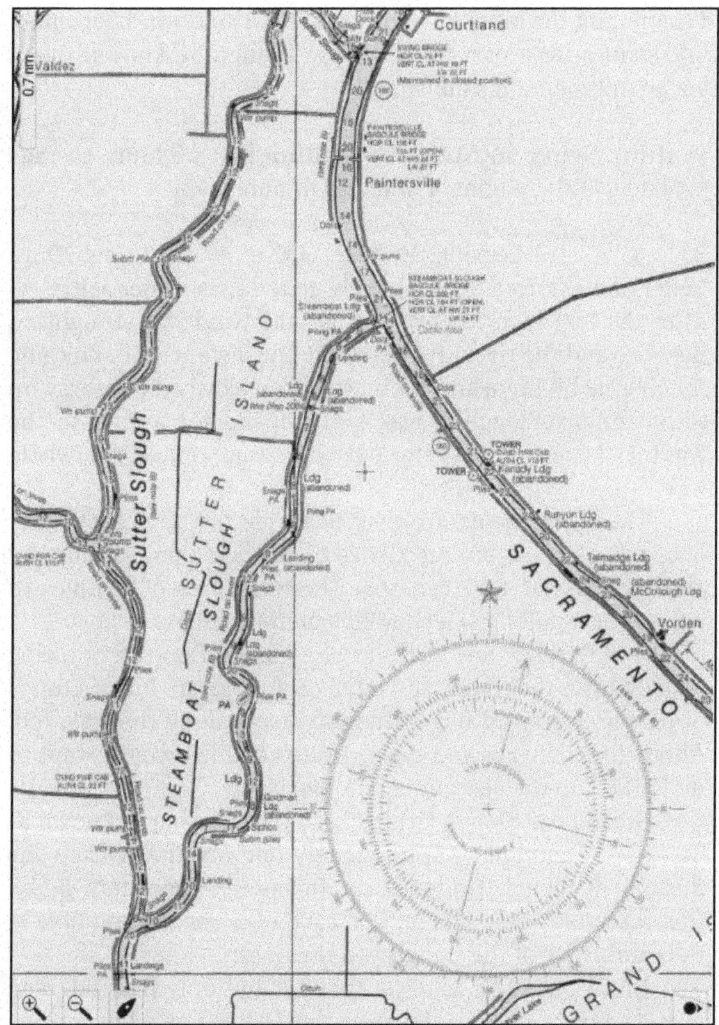

A number of families and lots of little children were just around the corner, under the Steamboat Slough Bridge at a small sandy beach. When I called the bridge operator on VHF channel 9 it was Demi again, who had been the Mokelumne Bridge operator the day before. She was very friendly and acknowledged my boat by name. I thanked her and she waved me through as she opened the bridge.

The wind had died, and from the bridge DM and I drifted down the slough in the ebb at 1.7 knots. We passed only one occupied sailboat, a boat with curvy, old fashioned lines. I waved as we drifted past and the people aboard stopped reading to wave back.

I floated down to get a sense of where to settle for the night. Keenly aware of my insufficient anchoring ability, I was lucky in my choice of neighbors. Sailing past a comfortable looking houseboat, I waved to its occupant, a woman who smiled and waved back.

The houseboat had a large patio and there was a second covered patio boat attached to its downstream end. Floating alongside were a small powerboat, a skiff with an outboard, a kayak and a seadoo. Most impressive was a lazyboy on the deck of the houseboat. There were four doggies, too.

I motored slowly back up the slough, close enough to introduce myself to Mary in the lazyboy. I asked her if she would mind if I anchored just below her and she called out, "Go right ahead!" And she smiled as if she meant it.

Boats anchored along Steamboat Slough

Then Mary called to her husband, Steve, who immediately climbed onto his seadoo and circled 'round as I headed up slowly and dropped my anchor well aft of their floating compound. Steve helped me by carrying my rear anchor further back of DM's stern after suggesting that I add more rode to it. Thank you, Sir. That was very kind of them both, and I hope to see them again one day.

8.12.19 Monday morning and at 8 am the sun has not yet cleared the trees. It is still shady but the water is moving fast. We are approximately one mile downriver from the Steamboat Slough Bridge, and the sounds that wake me are of farming equipment being either driven or towed along the levee road.

I can hear the clatter of large aluminum ladders bouncing in the truck beds toward the nearby fruit orchards. A tractor is carried past on a flatbed truck, an optimistic color of orange. It is new and shiny, a capital expense for the farmer and perfect for plowing fields that grow the fruit we all appreciate. Organic pears from the farm called Steamboat Acres.

The night before, there had been a fire on the levee. Mary asked me whether I heard all the noise of the firetrucks rushing by on the levee road just above our boats, but I hadn't. I slept right through all that excitement!

Mary waving from her houseboat

After breakfast, a bit of lounging and a quick dip in the cool water, I prepare to pull anchor and move on. It is 11 am as I wave goodbye and motor upstream briefly to thank Mary and Steve for their hospitality. I call across the water to ask Mary if her houseboat had a name.

"No, we just always called it the kids' playground. But they're all gone now and I kinda like it!" She gave a big grin and stretched out on the double lazyboy.

STEAMBOAT SLOUGH ANCHORAGE

8.12.19 Dura Mater and I are anchored along Steamboat Slough for a second night. I meant to turn to starboard at Cache Slough but we drifted blissfully past and missed it. Instead here we are, down near where Steamboat intersects with the Sacramento River's deep water channel. Farmland stretches into the distance on both sides.

At 7:30 pm it is 89 degrees. I'm too sweaty to drag a suit on so instead I take off my clothes and jump in the water in my underwear before I remember to be scared of the Delta pythons and hurry back up DM's stern ladder. Both ferries are broken ("non-functioning" is the Department of Transportation parlance), so there are no cars on the roads that run along either side of the slough. What are the roads? I have no idea. The Delta is mysterious that way. If you play along and don't use your laminated fishing map you are able to remain blissfully ignorant about your location.

Regardless of all that, we are here, floating on the water and the sunset is really pretty, so who cares? It is totally quiet except for thousands of birds and some kind of noisy frogs. Or maybe they are pythons calling to each other. Dinner is boat-temperature chicken noodle soup, rice crackers, cheddar cheese, and three bottles of water. There is no dessert because, of course, the chocolate had all melted.

8.13.19 During the night I listened to the occasional bump bump as small branches and waterlogged fruit carried by the ebbing tide landed against DM's stern. Bump. Bump.

They were gentle sounds, though unfamiliar, and unfamiliar sounds on a boat need to be addressed. It was almost a full moon with a cloudless sky so, when I climbed out in my nightshirt I was able to see clearly that no wild animals or boogie men were trying to board, so I crawled back down into the vberth and slept through the night until just before dawn.

Detritus at DM's stern

In the morning the sunrise was particularly pretty. Peeking over Dura Mater's transom, coffee cup in hand, I found a huge pileup of logs and branches and other kinds of flotsam against my stern. It looked like a beaver lodge.

What did I learn here? I learned that anchoring in a river or narrow slough is different than anchoring in an anchorage like Drakes Bay or a harbor at Half Moon Bay. In the Delta the flood currents are very brief and, especially in the springtime, the ebb is strong due to the runoff from upstream. Not thinking, I had anchored at both stern and bow, facing into the wind, not the inevitable ebb.

The aluminum plow anchor at our stern proved difficult to raise because it had caught on a sizable chunk of twisted tree root that was stuck somewhere down there in the water. It took such a long time and the day was getting warmer and warmer. I considered leaving it behind, but it is such a good anchor! That would just be wrong.

I gradually let out more and more line at the bow, until we were practically on top of it. I used the starboard self-tailing winch and it slowly and tortuously came up through the muddy water, along with a big chunk of the tree root. When I finally dislodged it from the anchor I felt like a dentist who had removed a difficult molar.

Turning to the Danforth at the bow, I needed to use DM's cabin top winch to pull it up, two torturous inches at a time: 80' of rode and 30' of chain. I sure wish I had a photograph of that tree root, but time was wasting and I didn't want to miss the 11 am - noon opening of the Rio Vista Bridge, which was my only choice absent a four hour call ahead window.

Rio Vista Bridge rising

Sailing through the bridge, Dura Mater and continued on to the Three Mile Slough Bridge and then to Owl Harbor for a few more days before heading back to Richmond.

Owl Harbor to Benicia 31.6 nm; 4.51 hours; 6.5 knots average

8.19.19 Another summer in the Delta is coming to an end for Dura Mater and me. The alarm goes off at 5:30 am and the sun is not up yet. At 6:04 am the wind is, according to my weather app, 7 mph wsw in Isleton. Leaving the mainsail covered, we leave the dock under motor at 6:25 am. There are already small white caps on the San Joaquin and at 7:15 am, it is still flooding. Our ETA to Benicia is 10:18 am and I think I might need to break out the ski goggles, so I put them on top of my head just in case. We pass five snowy egrets on Donlin Island @ 8:34 am.

The wind in Port Chicago Reach is 10-14 knots with higher gusts.

There was no attempt to sail during this trip. I got wet, though I have gotten wetter. There was no point in raising sail. You don't have to trust me on this. As Rob Tryon might say, "Try it yo own damn self!"

Benicia to Richmond 20.1 nm, 3 hours 10 minutes, 7.6 knot average

8.20.19 The next morning we left Benicia @ 6:55 am, arriving at Richmond Yacht Club harbor at 10:05 am on the ebb. We motored the whole way with a reefed main in case the wind came up fortuitously. It was a very fast return for us, due to the flat water and low wind. Thank goodness there was no drama during this trip.

What I have written here is what I learned by sailing my boat alone in the summer of 2019. Consider what you find here to be a series of observations, little adventures, stories written by an outsider. There were a few times when I motored, but for the most part I much preferred to sail, even very slowly. Before each little jaunt I would look in my tide book to see which way the currents would take us if we went that way, only to find that the tide was going that other way. Were Dura Mater and I willing to go that way? Well, maybe we were and maybe we weren't. A few times we went nowhere because it seemed more sensible to go swimming. Sometimes we got stuck in the mud and went nowhere at all. 2019 was another wonderful year in the Delta for Dura Mater and me.

SUMMER FOUR 2020

In July of 2017, when I made my first trip to the Delta, it was an idyllic experience. We had a gentle spinnaker run on a flood tide from Benicia all the way to Owl Harbor in Isleton. I couldn't stop taking photos so I would remember my experience, and in order to share it. Really, I was smitten.

Except for the trips home from the Delta to the San Francisco Bay, I was able to sail Dura Mater almost everywhere during the first three summers. Then, in 2020, we left the Bay for the Delta in early April rather than June or July. The sailing experience in early April of 2020 was remarkably different from my previous three visits to the Delta, and our Engine by Dave was used much more often.

I travelled some of the same routes, but because it was earlier in the year there was more water. Stronger water and lighter winds. I had learned to travel with the currents as much as possible. In April 2020, due to spring time runoff from the mountains, I was reminded of the sailor's adage "everything is the ebb, the ebb is everything" (Gordie Nash, SSS Three Bridge Fiasco skippers meeting, 2017).

Richmond Yacht Club harbor to Pittsburg Marina 5.5 hours, average 6.3 knots, 34.6 nm total.

4.12.20 On Easter Sunday 2020 @ 12:21 in the afternoon Dura Mater and I left Potrero Reach with the flood, motorsailing with a reefed main so the luff edge wouldn't catch on the backstay when we gybed. The top of the flood at Red Rock was noon.

We motorsailed the whole way, following along on the flood. At 1:52 pm there were whitecaps on the water and the boat slowed from 6.1 to 5.8 knots. It was hot in long sleeves but there was a small breeze from the west all the way across the San Pablo Bay, and we made good time.

We were still moving along well when we reached the Carquinez Bridge, so I decided not to stop in Benicia this year.

Benicia-Martinez Bridge

Once through the Benicia-Martinez Bridge we were in Bulls Head Channel, then East Bulls Head channel, then on to Preston Point Reach, keeping to the channel.

We stayed in Preston Point Reach, ignoring all those red and green channel markers way over there to starboard: that is Seal Island territory, where we got stuck in the mud during the Ditch Run in 2018. It's a restricted area.

After Preston Reach we entered Port Chicago Reach. The wind seems always to be strong through here. That is why the windsurfers love it. It's as windy as Anita Rock, sometimes more so. After Port Chicago Reach you are in the Suisun Bay and, yes, it just keeps getting windier and windier. It's because of that big fetch across Suisun, Grizzly and Honker Bays. There are windmills off to port here and as we approached Chipp's Island the water was increasingly boisterous.

At R "30" the choice was between starboard into New York Slough and on to the San Joaquin River, or straight ahead to the Deep Water Channel of the Sacramento River. Regardless of which way we go, the Pittsburg Marina is just around the corner to starboard. This year there were black sea lions lounging around on the buoys barking at us as I lowered the mainsail. Dura Mater hobby horsed in the waves that washed over her bow.

The wind was 18 knots with higher gusts and it had become really cold as we tucked into the Pittsburgh Yacht Club side of the Marina. I was relieved to be inside a harbor away from the impressive conditions just outside the seawall. I saw that the yacht club was closed up tight, the slips outside empty. There would be no hot shower for me this year, no reciprocity in the year of Covid, 2020.

In both the yacht club harbor and the public marina around the corner, the cost is the same for a slip: $0.50/foot per night. Put your cash into an envelope and then drop it into the box on the dock. Dura Mater is 27', so I paid $14 cash. Stagg chili for dinner, a few impressions in the notebook and then early to v-berth.

During each of the last three summers we sailed the whole way from the San Francisco Bay to Owl Harbor, but this year I felt an urgency to reach my destination.

Pittsburg Marina to Owl Harbor ~ 2.45 hours motorsailed in the flood

4.13.20 The next morning we exited the marina just before sunrise. At 6:05 am it was maximum flood into 14 knots of breeze.

Industrial landscape along Martinez

This is such a nice trip, especially before sunrise. The wind was 14 knots at the get-go and we left Pittsburg at 6:05 am. The industrial landscape along the San Joaquin looked completely different at daybreak.

Just before sunrise along the San Joaquin

2020 was the year of the Pandemic and I had a box of fresh masks aboard. I called ahead to Devery Stockon.

"Devery, if I promise to not touch anything and wear a mask, can I come to Owl Harbor and get a slip?"

"Yes"

"And I'm all out of eggs."

"We have eggs."

It was wool hat, wool socks, long underwear cold. We motorsailed the whole way and arrived at our assigned slip on I Dock in Owl Harbor @ 8:52 am. I was reminded again how enjoyable this trip is from Pittsburg onward, and how wonderful it is to sail anywhere, really, first thing in the morning.

SAILING WITHOUT PERMISSION IN 2020

4.14.20 After sleeping in, I sailed Dura Mater out of her slip on I dock at 12:25. The Humminbird informed me that it was only 4' deep at the entrance to Seven Mile Slough, so I felt lucky to get through.

Dura Mater and I exited Seven Mile slough, turned to starboard. The wind was about 8 knots. We don't have wind instruments, so I usually look it up afterwards and find that I had a general idea of the wind speed. It doesn't really matter to me how fast we go, only that we are back in the Delta.

We turned to port At Fishermans Cut, then right into False River, then left again and we sailed under little Frank's Tract. There was a comfortable wind that moved us along well, plus the ebb carried us. Curving down toward but not into Piper Slough, we meandered until the current changed, then turned around and, motorsailing when necessary, sailing when we were able, we continued along the top of Frank's Tract. Then we were on Old River, then Old River flats on the San Joaquin, then back to Owl Harbor.

Sailing time overall was 4.51 hours, we averaged 3.6 knots. The total trip was 17.4 nm. It was warm, 80 degrees, so I kept applying sunblock and drinking bottles of water. It was a lovely day and I was so happy to be back in the Delta.

CONCERT ON THE WATER

4.15.20 At 4:15 pm Dura Mater and I left our slip under sail. We exited Seven Mile Slough onto the San Joaquin and mostly just drifted down river. Over the next 2.5 hours we averaged 2.1 knots, over 5.19 nm. It was a leisurely and completely purposeless sail. I raised the black and yellow bumblebee drifter, tried to gybe it around the forestay but the bag and the extra lines kept catching. The spinnaker lines were as light as could be, but they were still too heavy for this evening's breeze. I tried to raise it with the spinnaker halyard, but that doesn't work because it's attached by its tack at the inside bottom of the forestay. Silly me.

It was such a nice night: balmy and pretty even with no wind. I ended up just lowering the drifter and shoving it into its bag on the cabin top in front of the mast. I lay back on it as DM and I drifted downwind with the ebb, steering the Pelagic with my remote doo hickey.

As the sun set we were surrounded by sound. To starboard were the sheep in the fields behind Owl Harbor. They were calling to the sea lions over on the Webb Tract, who were very excited. First the sheep would make a great racket, then they would stop. Then the sea lions would respond noisily, then stop. Back and forth. Back and forth. I swear they were communicating. Dura Mater and I just floated along. Pier 39 meets the Delta. Then we headed back to our slip. It was a great show.

BRIDGE INOPERABLE

4.16.20 The plan for today was to sail from Owl Harbor, up Three Mile Slough to the Sacramento River, under the Rio Vista Bridge, on to Cache Slough then to anchor in Prospect Slough. I had read a Latitude 38 article from 2011 about Prospect Slough.

This is what LaDonna Buback wrote:

Situated just off Cache Slough where it connects to the Sacramento Deep Water Channel, Prospect Slough's abundant trees provided scenery, shade and wind protection, as well as habitat for any number of bugs and the birds that eat them.

This sounded very appealing, so Prospect Slough was our destination.

A year or so ago the Rio Vista Bridge was inoperable for a period of time, which meant that I didn't sail up that way. This time I called the Rio Vista Bridge operator directly. I told him that I would be sailing from Owl Harbor and he assured me that the Rio Vista Bridge was indeed working. All I had to do, he said, was call on Channel 9.

I checked the Delta currents: at 7 am the next morning it would be slack tide at the intersection of the San Joaquin and Three Mile Slough, starting to flood. I set the alarm for 5:30. My intention was to motor out of Seven Mile Slough, turning to starboard into the San Joaquin in time to feel the warmth of the sun as it came up behind us.

The next morning we left the dock @ 6:15 am just before the sun came up. I love to start sailing this early, but no matter how early DM and I get out there, fishermen are already on the water: In the sloughs, between the tule islands, everywhere around corners of the San Joaquin River. They are patient and courteous and sometimes they will even wave back. I suspect they roll their eyes at recreational sailors. I mean, seriously? What's the point if you don't get to take anything home to eat? I get it.

At first it all went according to plan. I was enjoying my second cup of coffee, putting along. As we approached Three Mile Slough Bridge I called the bridge operator on Channel 9:

"Three Mile Slough Bridge, this is the sailing vessel Dura Mater approaching from the east, do you copy?"

There was a long pause. I tried again.

"Three Mile Slough Bridge, this is the sailing vessel Dura Mater approaching from the east. Could you please open for us?"

Long minutes later someone finally came on the radio to inform me that the Three Mile Slough bridge would not open. It hadn't been operable for some time and no one seemed to know when it would open again.

This was an unexpected situation. I was all stocked and bundled up with nowhere to go. I knew what my options were, but they weren't very attractive. I could motorsail all the way back down the San Joaquin, circle Sherman Island then motorsail back up the Sacramento. Huh. That itinerary was not in my head. Instead I turned around and sailed back down the slough.

By the time I reached the San Joaquin there was a gentle breeze coming directly behind us so of course I raised the spinnaker. Just as soon as it was up the wind clocked around and there we were on a beam reach with the spinnaker still up. We flew upriver toward the Delta Loop.

There were two fellas anchored in their small boat with their fishing poles out. They watched me as I passed by, Pelagic maintaining our course. It was getting too hot to be moving around so much anyway, so I circled around Channel marker #44 slowly, still using my remote.

While I was shoving the spinnaker down DM's forward hatch, we passed the fishermen again, going the other way. I looked down at them as we passed within a boat's length. Neither of them had moved. One of them grinned up at me and called up:

"So now do you raise it again to go back the other way?" I could tell that he knew the answer.

"No, I don't think it would work that way!" We both laughed.

Dura Mater is in the Delta again and she galumphs along easily in these waters, with no need to compare herself to faster, sleeker boats. She and I tacked our way downriver, home to Seven Mile Slough and Owl Harbor, back in our slip @ 11:23 am. Disappointment was replaced by a nice wind, the red white and blue of my spinnaker and the pleasant interaction with a complete stranger on the water. Moving time was 5:09 hrs. 22.2 nm total.

MEETING THE NEIGHBORS

4.16.20 What does the Delta look like during the Great Pandemic of 2020? The sky is still blue, the herons are still annoyed with the humans and the grasses still sway in the wind. People are sensible here. They keep their distance, but still smile, as Delta people tend to do. And in April? It's still a bit chilly at night, but today it was warm enough for the chocolate to soften.

The wind comes from different directions in April than during the summer, just as it does in the Bay Area. Mount Diablo is always there in the distance, across the alfalfa fields along Owl Harbor's gardens and clearly visible all along the San Joaquin River.

After exerting myself during the morning I take a nap, read a book, take another nap. Then I ate dinner: scrambled eggs and Havarti cheese. Here at Owl Harbor the eggs are not as plentiful as in years past, since a raccoon has gotten into the coop and killed 16 chickens. Eggs are still available on a first come first served basis though, and I snagged a few. Then there is the whole egg shortage in the stores issue, reflecting the pandemic. I'll never take eggs for granted again.

There I am, scrubbing eggs from the frying pan in my little galley sink, when I look out my companionway to see three singlehanders come back in from sailing! 17 knots of wind in the early evening! They all turn in to their slips on the dock next door: H dock seems to be racer's dock at Owl Harbor. I walk over.

"Hi, guys!" They were nice as could be. Joyful, even, as sailors tend to be everywhere after racing around on the water.

There is a Newport 30, a Nonsuch 30, then a Newport 28. Right next to each other! Turns out they all come down to their boats Thursday night and sail around out on the San Joaquin River. Do they race? Nah. Nothing like that. They just follow each other around.

Will they be here next Thursday? Sure! What a coincidence. So will Dura Mater! We all agreed that singlehanded sailing is essential to our wellbeing.

KEEPING UP WITH THE NEIGHBORS

4.23.20 I drove home to Oakland for a couple of days, then returned the following Thursday. When I arrived, I drove slowly slowly along the gravel road above the water of Seven Mile Slough. You must drive slowly slowly at Owl Harbor or you get into trouble. Looking down from the levee road I saw my neighbors on H dock preparing their boats, so I rolled down my car window and called out:

"What time are we going out?"
"Four O clock," someone called up to me.
"Excellent!"

I parked my car on the grass, ran up the hill, down the ramp to I Dock and jumped aboard Dura Mater. I raised her sail, putting in a reef because it was windy, and we followed them out, slowly and under motor. I hoped they had deeper drafts than ours, because it can get really shallow at the entrance to Seven Mile Slough.

I learned about Seven Mile Slough un-race etiquette, and the intricacies of civil sailing society. This is how it works: Everybody lets the Newport 30 lead the way from Seven Mile Slough into the River. It has a wing keel, and that keel carves a path through the choking grasses for the rest of us. The Newport is the sacrificial boat and also the leader of the pack.

Once you get through the entrance it's a good idea to put your engine in reverse and go backward and forward a couple of times in order to shake off as much foliage as you can. What kind of foliage? I have no idea. It grows in the water and fakes out the depth finder. Sometimes it reads nine feet, then three feet. Sailing out of Owl Harbor is a surprise and an adventure every time you leave and return to the Slough.

Once we're all on the River the other boats raised their sails. I followed a new-to-me yellow hull as it sailed downriver/upwind. After a bit the fella turned around and headed back, drifting close to Dura Mater in the flood. Our boats were close to each other and I called out:

"Are you going back in?"

"No. There's another boat coming out. I'm waiting." He smiled over at me.

So there was. I watched as the fifth boat emerged from Seven Mile Slough. Local etiquette requires everyone to wait until all sails are raised. Alrighty, then. Now we know.

Well, once we had all raised our sails in the San Joaquin River, the hell it wasn't a race! They were off, into the white caps and against the building flood. I tried to keep up, and they tried to shake me. At least that's how it seemed. They went through Santa Clara shoal. I followed. They turned to port past Bradford Island. I followed. Tack, tack and tack again.

We were shoved sideways by the wind to begin with, and further sideways by the flood. An hour into the non race we had sailed only 2.6 miles. These Delta sailors, they really know how to tack. I notice that a lot of sailboats in the Delta have adapted to the environment and have rigged their boats so the jibs self-tack. They kept looking back to see if I was keeping up. With my non-self-tacking boat? I was sure trying.

Singlehanded racing on the San Joaquin

The wind was 15 knots gusting to over 20. It was SO MUCH FUN! We finally circled green channel marker #25 to starboard, than headed back toward the colored sky of sunset. We all waved goodnight and turned to the task of putting our boats and ourselves to bed for the night.

Owl Harbor to Disappointment Slough 10:25 am - 3:35 pm. 10.9 nm, Moving average 2.5 knots, wind 10 knots.

How do I choose to sail somewhere? There are so many beautiful places from which to choose. I have heard the same names over and over: Georgiana Slough, Steamboat Slough, The Bedrooms. And yes, they are beautiful waterways. I'd heard all about them before I arrived and they didn't disappoint.

But I like going to places that I've never heard people mention. The slough less travelled, if you will. Which is one reason why I decided to sail to Disappointment Slough. It was also difficult to resist the name.

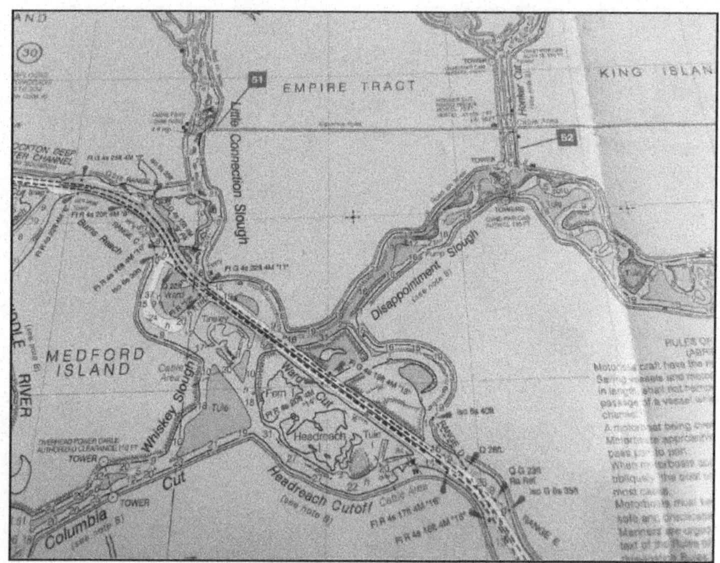

Chart of Disappointment Slough

In his book Dawdling on the Delta, Hal Schell had this to say about my next destination: “On dark, moonless nights, or during times of heavy tule fogs, the gentle bend of Disappointment Slough was easily confused for the river itself. Thus, disgruntled riverboat pilots gave the slough its name.” I consider whether Disappointment Slough will disappoint me?

4.25.20 On this Saturday morning, shortly after exiting Seven Mile Slough, I raise the spinnaker. As DM and I sail slowly past the entrance to the Mokelumne River and then Potato Slough, the San Joaquin fills with dozens of power boats passing us by on either side. It is difficult to keep the spinnaker full of wind because of all their wakes. It is the weekend and there is every type of boat on the water: long lean boats with flames along their hulls, power boats pulling kids on colorful donuts and fast low boats pulling adults on skis. There are lots of couples on Sea Doos leaping up out of the water, pontoon boats over in the sloughs and pretty little cabin cruisers full of large families.

We are the only sailboat on the River.

We turn to port into Disappointment Slough and drop the spinnaker. There are some gusts, then the wind calms down a bit as we sail slowly toward King's Marina, which has gas but no diesel. Transient slips are advertised, but I don't know that they are meant for keelboats because my depth finder tells me that the water turns shallow quickly, down to 7' in the approach to the fuel dock.

The chart plotter is not helpful here and I'm reminded of Tom Patterson's advice. He told me:

> "Don't believe the depths on the chart ... the only thing that has been surveyed are the channels. None of the rest of this stuff has been surveyed."

According to my paper boating chart there is ice and bait to be had at King's Marina, but I don't think I can get close enough to buy either. It has been a long, hot day. A cold drink sure would be nice. I ask myself, "Jackie, are you feel lucky today?" and pivot away instead.

After anchoring twice along one of the main arteries of Disappointment, I decide to tuck into one of the cross sloughs instead and we settle in. Anchoring and re-anchoring was hot work and at 5 pm it is still 88 degrees here.

Looking up, I find that we are right beneath an enormous power tower with a huge nest at the very top. There is also a huge bird up there. Really big, even from this distance. Lucky me I have new binocs, a birthday present to myself. That bird up there guarding that nest doesn't like the idea that Dura Mater and I will be staying the night. I could tell that its aggressive sounds are meant for us because, well, we're the only ones here.

Aside from the San Joaquin, which is a main drag for boat racing, Disappointment Slough seems to be another venue for fast boats that like to zig and zag. As I eat my dinner in the cockpit I watch them as they race by on the fairways to each side of where we are anchored in our own shallow and sluggish slough. The sunset is an incredible orange and red and gold.

I realize that I am very tired and besides, I had to pull up that chain and anchor twice. We are anchored in about 14' with 30 ' chain and 50' rode. After trying and failing to figure out the anchor alarm on my handheld Garmin, I turn it off. There is neither wind nor waves. I'm pretty sure we are stuck like glue.

As darkness falls I look up, and the bird is still on its nest, its beak averted, disdainful, standing sentinel. I turn on the masthead anchor light and now I finally crawl into the v berth. As I start to fall asleep I hear the sound of a fast boat approaching, people laughing. A girl screams, "Look out!" as they fly over my anchor line. I conclude that boats don't usually anchor here.

After waiting for the wake to settle, I climb out of my v berth, go over to my switches and turn on every one of Dura Mater's lights. On go the running lights and her offshore tricolor mast head light. Then I put fresh batteries into the battery operated lantern, go out in my nightshirt and hang it from my bow pulpit. Next summer I'm bringing Christmas lights to string along the lifelines. Call it defensive space.

Disappointment Slough to Mildred Island 10.4 nm 3:44 hrs

4.26.20 When I wake up the next morning @ 5:30 am, the first thing I do it look to see that huge bird still up there. There must be eggs in the nest rather than baby birds, otherwise the bird would be off looking for food, right? Babies would require fussing. The tower is so high that I can't get a good look at the bird and there's no one around to ask whether it's a hawk or another kind of bird.

Disappointment Slough hasn't disappointed me at all. It doesn't take long to pull anchor and it comes up along with a ton of mud and foliage. Everything is spattered with mud, including me.

Exiting Disappointment Slough we sail upriver on the San Joaquin and then turn to starboard at Headreach Cutoff. It's shallow at the entrance and the fish finder goes crazy, but we persevere and once past that shoal spot it's very pretty. At starboard it looks like the Everglades, but with all the wrong trees. A family of pelicans sits on rotten logs, watching us, and then there are lovely homes with docks that beckon. But not to us.

If you follow this waterway 'round and off to starboard you'll find yourself in one of the two Whiskey Sloughs. Why are there two, in completely different locations? I have no idea. The linguistic mysteries of the Delta continue to delight. We sail on down Columbia Cut and down Latham Slough, passing by the Five Fingers because all five are full of flat bottomed fishing boats and there are birds standing around. We know the drill.

Finally we arrive at Mildred Island.

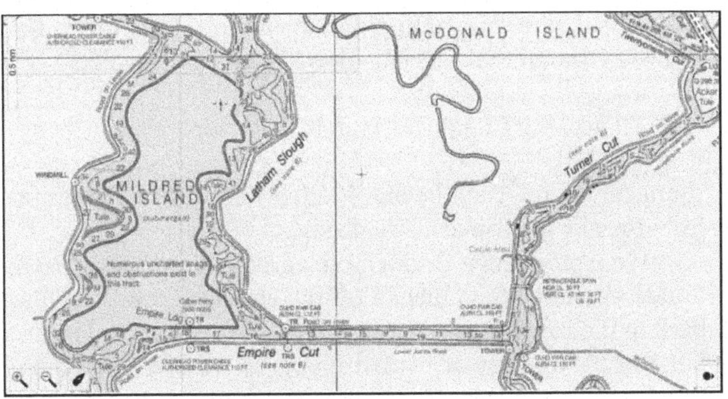

Not an island at all, it is now a large lake. On the way here the wind was wnw, about 10 knots with periodic higher gusts. Even with wind shifts it was mostly a beam reach the whole way from the San Joaquin.

When we finally entered Mildred Island we criss-crossed it several times, keeping an eye on the depth finder. It is approximately 16' almost everywhere at low tide. I jury rigged a bridle for the anchor rode at Dura Mater's bow, swung wide back and forth until I got a little nauseous, took a bonine and crawled into the v-berth for a nap. Why not? I was hot and it wasn't dinner time yet.

It was an uneventful night and the next morning we left Mildred Island @ 10:20 am. It took awhile to remove the debris and mud from the anchor. Again.

Mildred Island to Owl Harbor 20.3 nm 5:10 hrs

4.27.20 Exiting Mildred Island into Empire Cut, we drifted along fast in the ebb until we had to make a decision between north and south. First we went south, then north into some shallow tules. After pivoting away out of the increasingly shallow water, we approached Turner Cut Bridge by another approach. Really? I had no idea where we were. I turned on the engine finally and called the bridge operator on channel 9. His response?

"Sailboat, I saw you coming and opened up the bridge, then you went 'round that tule island so I closed it up again."

"Oh! Thank you! Could you open it again, please?"

"Sure. Hold on." Then he did. From now on Dura Mater and I feel officially identified as "Sailboat".

We motor sailed through the narrow space, waved to the bridge operator, then turned off the engine and sailed slowly back to the San Joaquin in the ebb. There were some big gusts but mostly we sort of drifted along. It was real pretty and there were hundreds of egrets everywhere. It was egret heaven. They own the place.

There are lots of birds everywhere in the Delta. Lots and lots of birds, and especially egrets. In Turner Cut I saw a mother egret with about 5 babies floating along behind. Along Empire Cut just out of Mildred Island I watched an egret mama teach her baby how to fly, first flying ahead, then stopping on the rip rap waiting for her young one to catch up. The mother's aerodynamics were impressive and she needed to flap many fewer times than did the baby.

Mama egret: Flaaaap. Flaaaap. Lands. Looks back. Waits patiently. Repeats.

Young egret: flapflapflapflapflapflapflap. Catches up to the mama. Repeats.

Up the entire long slough they went. They were still teaching and learning as we drifted out of sight in the other direction.

According to the signs, Turner Cut Marina has gas for sale but no diesel. The ebb was a strong 2.91 knots and it moved us right along, back to the San Joaquin River, where the ebb grew so that our return to Owl Harbor under sail was a 3.9 average.

We arrived at Seven Mile Slough at 3:30 pm at low tide and I felt lucky to get through the entrance with its notorious eel grass. Showering in Owl Harbor's wonderful clubhouse felt particularly satisfying.

CHASING THE NEIGHBORS

5.7.20 Two Thursdays later, this week's non-race on the San Joaquin River had five boats chasing each other around again. We headed down river and upwind until the wind clocked around 180 degrees and then everybody turned one by one to head the other way. Toward Stockton. Which is up river. Yeah. That Up River/Down River business is a little confusing for the first four years. Having left the dock @ 4 pm we returned just as the sun was setting across the alfalfa fields. The wind wasn't so strong this week, none of us had reefed, and one fella even switched his jib out for a really big one.

The sails on Up Delta boats aren't fancy racing sails. In fact, they're kinda soft looking. Not crisp, fancy black ones made from high tech materials that are more common on San Francisco Bay. At the end of the race everybody circles around off Seven Mile Slough until all boats have taken their sails down and are ready to return to port. Mark explained later that they all wait for each other as a courtesy: No boat left behind.

After the un-race I left my sails in a mess and walked over to H Dock. Trying to put their boats to bed before the bugs descended, they were all flaking their sails and drinking beer. I stood on the dock between the boats and asked how they are able to choose the perfect course that offers wind the entire time, and a return to harbor before the sun sets?

Randy of the Newport 28 responded in highly technical sailboat racing terms:

"Well, we can either turn right or left," said Randy.

Sailors around here describe their courses by local channel markers, not buoys or landmarks. Did he remember where we had turned around? He considered for a moment, counting to himself:

"Markers 57, 58," he said.

When I looked at the chart later I saw that we had sailed just past Prisoners Point, turning between, yep, channel markers 57 and 58. Indelicately I asked about the sails on Randy's boat: "How old is your mainsail?"

Randy looked over at Mark on his Nonsuch.

R: "When did I buy this boat from you?"

M: "You bought it from me six years ago. But I bought it in 2004 with those sails."

R: "Isn't this mainsail great? It has full battens and still has its shape."

M: "That IS still a great mainsail. Given its age."

They grinned like goofs. UpDelta sailors are happy with the boats they got.

It was another lovely night. T-shirt weather from start to finish, and then a scramble to put up the bug screen as night fell in Owl Harbor.

THE DELTA TUNNELS

Long before I ever visited the Delta, back when I lived in New York City, I read a series of news articles about the Twin Tunnels. The tone of some of the articles suggested that opposition to the tunnels was a matter of local ignorance. Other views were that water for the rest of California was being held hostage by whacky environmentalists on behalf of small frogs. People were suffering during droughts and it was all because those crazy obstructionists were protecting the smelt. What was a smelt? Who knew?

Then I moved back to Oakland, started asking questions, and the arguments became a bit more nuanced. Not just the frogs or the smelt, but a whole farming community, depended upon that water. Fishing and recreational boating communities shared 1000 miles of waterways. And birds! There are so many species of birds that depend upon the marshlands and slow moving sloughs. A way of life is held in the balance, an hour away yet even further in mindset from the urbanity of the San Francisco Bay area.

During the past several years, the argument in favor of taking water from the Delta has been repackaged. The Twin Tunnels are now in the rear view mirror and the argument has transmogrified. The effort to divert water from the upper Sacramento River is now referred to as The Water Conveyance.

Those who do not agree with this version of the story are seen as willfully obdurate. But the arguments in favor of conveying Delta water out seem to be in stark conflict with officials in place whose responsibility it is to protect and manage the water supply.

For example, here is an excerpt from the Central Delta Water Agency's Comments on the "Notice of Preparation of Environmental Impact" with regard to the Delta Conveyance Project:

> *Needless to say the proposed project is a complete disaster in the making for the Delta and the worst possible alternative to address the paramount co-equal goals of "providing a more reliable water supply for California and protecting, restoring, and enhancing the Delta ecosystem." (Wat. Code, § 85054.)*
>
> *The proposed project simply could not fall any further short of the mandate that the coequal goals shall be achieved in a manner that protects and enhances the unique cultural, recreational, natural resource, and agricultural values of the Delta as an evolving place. April 17, 2020.*

The more I read the more confusing it became. I am a simple person who enjoys sailing in quiet, unpolitical water. Before heading to the Delta in 2020 I decided to call Bill Wells, head of the Delta Chamber of Commerce.

Bill was as nice as could be, and the first question he asked was: "What kind of boat do you have?" Now, in my opinion this is the best kind of question one person can ask of another, and it establishes the ground rules for the future of your relationship with each other.

Bill described himself as "a sailor at heart", though his current boat, Ranger, has no mast, no sails. Built in 1937, Ranger is a classic 36' Stephens motor yacht. Testing the parameters of our future boat friendship, I suggested that his boat might be a bit more comfortable than my own. He reluctantly agreed. "Well ... maybe." See how nice he is?

Ranger on Georgiana Slough

Bill is also the editor of Bay and Delta Yachtsman magazine. Originally a tabloid paper printed in Rio Vista, the Yachtsman started in 1965. Bill came to my attention as an outspoken opponent of the Delta Tunnels. I've been reading his articles since I first visited the Delta in 2017.

INTERVIEW WITH BILL WELLS

On May 16, 2020 I drove my car from Owl Harbor to meet Bill and Sue Wells outside the Oxbow Marina office. We sat on the patio in the shade and chatted about water and boats. Here is what Bill had to say.

Bill: *We've lived in Sacramento since 1975 and I bought this boat in 1993. So I've had it for about twenty five years or more. I've cruised around the Delta a lot since then. Cruising season around here is generally from May to Labor Day but frankly I like to extend it out to November. To me, that's the best time: from September through November, when it starts cooling off. In a power boat you're inside so you can pretty much powerboat all year.*

I still enjoy gunkholing, seeing how far I can go up some little slough without running aground and wrecking my boat. I draw about 30 inches, kind of like a centerboard sailboat, maybe. To me, Georgiana Slough is the most beautiful waterway in the whole Delta. You've got all the trees overhanging and you see quite a bit of wildlife. And Steamboat Slough is really beautiful too.

I asked Bill about his opinion of the Delta Tunnels, and this is what he told me:

Regarding the water tunnels: Jerry Brown, back in the early 1980s, wanted to build a peripheral canal and coincidentally a lot of the farmers in the central valley didn't want to do it because they thought it was some kind of scam on his part to not give them any water. The peripheral canal went to the voters and was defeated.

Then Arnold Schwarzenegger, approximately fifteen years ago, announced that he wanted to have a "conveyance" and announced it to the farmers down in the Westlands water district, which is the desert in the San Joaquin Valley. We've been fighting that ever since Schwarzenegger went out of office. Originally

Schwarzenegger was going to promote a canal, then ... they switched from a canal to these twin tunnels.

When Schwarzenegger first announced that he wanted to divert the river the Delta Chambers took a position that we would oppose that. Virtually all our members are in favor of us opposing it.

Faded poster in a downtown window, Rio Vista

We spent ten years fighting that and won and showed them that's not a good idea. The people in the Delta stood up and defeated the twin tunnel plan. That was a year ago and then Gavin Newsom comes on board. Originally we thought he was going to be on our side. Then he announced this single tunnel idea. It's not really how many tunnels or canals you have, it's how much water you export from the Delta. We figure you can export maybe 3 million acre feet of water per year, they're up to five million right now and they're looking at 10 or more if they build this "conveyance".

I was actually with the chamber first, then the publishers of Bay and Delta Yachtsman asked me if I would do a temporary column and I said, "Yes". Then they came to me after a few issues and asked if I would write a monthly column about "politics" and "boating", so I [understood] "politics" to mean fighting the water tunnels. I've been doing that since 2010, 2011, something like that.

Prominent sign at Pirates Lair Marina, Isleton

That's where we're at. We've been actively fighting Newsom and his tunnel thing. There are two water projects: one is the federal Central Valley Project and the other is the State Water Project. One federal and one state. Generally they work together to try and take as much water as possible. Ultimately, I'm confident they're not going to build any diversion to move the river around the Delta because it's a stupid idea [Bill laughs, shaking his head]. *At some point common sense will prevail, I'm sure.*

Jackie: My understanding from Devery Stockon, at Owl Harbor, is that a lot of this land is leased to farmers. Is it privately owned or is it owned by the state and leased long term to the farmers? What is your understanding?

B: *It's mostly fee simple, you own it. It's just like when you buy a house, you buy the lot that's it's on, that's fee simple. Versus leasehold where you might have a 99 year or 55 year lease, something like that. I'm pretty sure most of the land in the Delta is actually owned by the people. I think.*

Posted sign on Twitchell Island

J: So all this beautiful farmland, all these crops and orchards are owned by the farmers?

B: *As far as I know, there are a lot of farmers that actually own the land.*

J: Then how can the state do that?

B: *They claim that they've got the right to do it. We've been fighting them for years over that and they constantly come back. Some law back in the 60s, they say they can divert as much water as they want. On the other hand, the North Delta Water agency was promised to keep their water quality the same, i.e. you can't let more salt water intrude up into the Delta. That's carved in granite but the State of California is trying to get around that.*

Bumper sticker in restaurant window, Walnut Grove

The State of California made that commitment to them and it's in writing. This goes back before my time, back into the early or mid 60s. When they were working on the original peripheral canal or thinking about doing something. A lot of farmers and land owners are up in that area: Clarksburg and Courtland and Hood, that area.

Not all pear farmers, there are grapes up there, a lot of pears, too. Pears, from what I gather, are fairly [sensitive] to salt water intrusion, so it doesn't take much salt water to mess up pears. People in Clarksburg, they're all fighting the tunnels. Going to meetings, speaking out, chipping in to hire Michael Brodsky as a lawyer. He lives in Discovery Bay part time but his office is in Santa Cruz.

Sherman Island, which you cruise by when you sail up here, originally there was a lot of asparagus grown there. In the years since they started exporting more and more water from the Delta the salt water started intruding more up there. So the State bought most of Sherman Island and now it's just used for dredger spoils. They might grow alfalfa or something like that, but they can't grow asparagus there any more.

J: How does that happen?
B: *You've got the San Joaquin River and the Sacramento River flowing down into the Delta and then out to the Bay. The more water they take out of those two river systems, the farther the salt water intrudes up into the Delta. There's actually what they call the X-2 point, which is right around Pittsburg, down in the Benicia area.*

X-2 means two parts per sodium per thousand parts of water, they are not supposed to allow it to come any farther inland. It does change with the tides, naturally, and then winter versus summer. In the winter the x-2 point goes downstream quite a ways. In the summer it moves upstream.

J: So when you say, "They're not supposed to allow that", what you're saying is "They're not supposed to take so much water so that happens"?
B: *Right, the way water is exported right now, most of it does come out of the Sacramento River, but it goes either down Georgiana Slough, or up by Locke there's the Cross Channel Gate, a little dam, and they open that, which dumps into the Mokelumne River, and all that water ends up down in Tracy. That's where the pumps are and they pump it out. If those are going full blast, the flow to the Sacramento River is slowed down.*

Eddo's Harbor, which is on Sherman Island, is a big fishing resort. Chris Gulick is really concerned about the fish being killed off. It's not just the smelt, because other fish eat the smelt. That's just one tiny little factor. All of the fish would suffer, farmers too. Laura Scheidegger has a farm on Twitchell Island.

J: What do they grow?

B: *Stone fruit, which is any fruit with a hard pit in the center. I've got a friend, Arnold Strecker, who is an alfalfa farmer down on King Island, down by Stockton.*

J: What do they say? Have they been affected already?

B: *Yeah, not as bad as they're going to be if they ever go to fruition with this [water conveyance plan], but definitely. Even Stockton, they built their city water intake right on the San Joaquin River, so that's at risk now if the salt comes farther up that way.*

The San Joaquin is already diverted quite a bit. I can't think of the name of the dam, but they take a lot of the water out of the San Joaquin River and use it in the farms, then they recycle it by pumping it back into the river. The land down there has a lot of selenium and pesticides so it's not really clear, pure water coming down the San Joaquin River as much as it is the Sacramento River.

Bill, Sue and I shook our heads at the futility of trying to change the world. Then we laughed, looked around at the beautiful day and realized we could talk about boats some more instead.

J: Last year, when I sailed up Georgiana ... I pulled up my anchor and it was full of those Quagga mussels! My Danforth was full of mud and it was crammed full of those mussels. I was a little startled. Big ones, little ones, the little ones the size of my thumbnail, bigger ones.

B: *On your boat, [quaggas] attach themselves to the propeller and these IO boats they have the thing that tilts up and down? The propeller? They crawl inside of there and they grow and jam up the mechanism. It's terrible. Then down where they have water pumps, that pump water to farms? They get inside the pumps and grow in there. I've never seen it up here but I've seen pictures of them elsewhere: a huge knot of them inside things. The shells are calciumso it basically breaks the pump.*

J: So that's why they don't want them up here? They can break mechanisms?
B: *They'll clog up any kind of thing that transports water. And they'll even get into the intake to your motor. The main thing I've heard about them is they destroy farming machinery.*

J: What does the Delta Chamber of Commerce do for businesses?
B: *Anything we can possibly do. [laughs] We've got about 200 members and an active website. We have about 400,000 visitors a year to the website, people looking to come here. People call about restaurants all the time. There are plenty of great places to eat in the Delta. Anybody who calls or mentions the word 'Delta', somehow the call gets routed to us. I get a lot of calls. Sailors coming up: 'I'm sailing up the San Joaquin River, I'm completely lost! There are all these channels!'*

So I ask, "Do you see any landmarks?"
'Yeah, there's tules all around me.'

Bill laughs.

Sometimes I can get 'em to mention a buoy. On my bedroom wall at home I've got Hal Schell's old map pinned up there, it's still got the buoys on it. When I first pinned it up there I'd have to run in there and look, but now I can fairly much do it off the top of my head.

Bill, Sue and I laugh and laugh together. It feels nice to be meeting somewhere in person again, after so many months of careful distancing due to the covid pandemic. We realize that boat stories never end, we could tell them all day long. But Bill and Sue? They have places to go, things to do and people to see. They leave in their air conditioned car and I go inside the marina office for an ice cream bar.

Owl Harbor to Oxbow Marina 10:45 am – 2:13 pm

5.19.20 The Mokelumne River Bridge is open again after a long time closed. When DM and I arrived at 2:13 pm today it wasn't very windy, but it is forecast to pick up, maybe even gust to 30 knots. I am not yet confident about anchoring and don't want to be caught off guard, so I decide to pay for a slip and stay the night.

After taking a hot shower I settle in for the evening in Dura Mater's cabin, eating Campbells chicken noodle soup and rice crackers. The wind outside the Marina has built to 17 knots but here we are protected, surrounded by the tall palm trees for which Oxbow is known. There are the low reeds along the slough just the other side of the marina entrance, and farmland all around.

Over the years I have considered how it must be to sail across the Pacific to Hawaii. It would be terrifying for me. In total darkness? Never stopping? In high wind and waves? Oh. My. God. That is a whole lot of scary. I don't know how people do it. Give me the slow moving water of the Delta, an anchor with 30' of chain and lots of batteries for my headlamps. That's as brave as I get.

The itinerary for tomorrow is to continue on along Georgiana Slough, through the Tyler Island Bridge under the Georgiana Slough Bridge and then to Walnut Grove, maybe stop in to say "hello" to James Whitaker, the bridge operator there.

Oxbow Marina to Georgiana Anchorage 8.16 nm; 3:31 hrs. 2.3 knot average

052020 Since last year's anchoring fiasco here on Georgiana Slough I have spent some time reading up on the topic. What had I done wrong? Had I done anything right? Nothing in print regarding anchoring is particularly helpful to a singlehander. Why is that? I had no idea.

Before leaving Owl Harbor I walked over to my Delta guru's boat. Rob Tryon had just installed air conditioning in his own yacht. He and his girl were laying around in chilly splendor like cats full of canaries and it was hard to get him to focus at first. But Rob is an excellent sailor and a singlehander, too. I knew I could count on him. He said:

"It's simple, Jackie. Pick your spot. Drop one anchor at the stern with a lot of rode, motor forward until you run out of rode. Drop the other anchor at the bow. Drift back or motor slowly, taking up the slack in the rode at the stern until you run out of rode at the bow. Or do it backwards. Whichever works best for you. Got it?"

I thought I did. "*G'won, then.*" Rob shooed me away with both arms and a big grin.

A complicating factor in the Delta is the fact that the wind and currents often work against the sailor as she tries to anchor. This year, in the spring time, the wind might be adequate but the ebb is always stronger than mere adequate wind. I should have paid attention to Jonathan Gutoff.

"It's always ebbing on Georgiana even when it's flooding," Jonathan had reminded me. He was so right.

Silos along Georgiana Slough

Leaving Oxbow at 11:50 am, I was determined to fly a spinnaker as I had done the year before in mid-August. I had enjoyed myself so much and so effortlessly!

We motorsailed out of Oxbow and started up Georgiana Slough. Alright, I'll admit it, this route does have pretty scenery.

Once through Tyler Island Bridge the wind was behind us as I raised the spinnaker, but even so Dura Mater and I were going nowhere fast. As the ebb increased, I remained determined. I was huffing and puffing in the heat, flailing from side to side in the narrow slough, but it was no use. We were actually drifting backwards, spinnaker full.

Some fellas were sitting in camp chairs, fishing along the edge of the Slough to our starboard side. They watched us motor past, then watched us again as we floated back downstream.

The bridge operator back at the Tyler Island Bridge hailed us on Channel 9: "Sailboat, I see you coming back this way. Do you want me to open up the bridge for you again?"

"No need," I replied. "I give up."

It was disheartening to move around so much for so little effect, but I went up to the bow, stuffed the spinnaker down the hatch and then turned on our Engine by Dave. The fishermen waved as we passed them by for the third time. What had I learned today? Even a decent wind at the top of Dura Mater's mast cannot begin to compete with the ebb tide dragging her fat little stern down river.

As we continued up Georgiana, I recalled Richard the Kayaker's advice and located a tree-less mud bank less than a mile south of Georgiana Slough Bridge. Rob's method requires a good long bit of bare space along a waterway, because trees and standing rigging do not get along well.

After dropping the stern anchor (my plow anchor) I motored forward slowly up current until it caught and I couldn't go forward any more. Then, using Pelagic, I went forward and dropped the danforth at the bow. That done, I went back to the cockpit and put the engine in neutral, drifting back and taking in the stern anchor rode until the bow anchor caught. And presto! We were anchored by 3:34 pm, snugged up at each end and having done a damned fine job of it, too.

This year we are in the Delta during April and May and there have been no mosquitoes. Seriously? Yes: No Mosquitoes. That doesn't mean there are no bugs. Oh, there are bugs. It is cool at night and I leave my companionway and forward hatch open so I can listen to the trees' branches as they brush against each other in the breeze. I listen to the frogs in the mud next to us on our own muddy little beach. And to the bugs.

I like listening to the bugs but I don't want to share my cabin with them, so this is what I do: I buy narrow strips of sticky-back Velcro and apply it to the inside edges of DM's companionway entry and forward hatch. Then I buy the prettiest tulle material I can find at a fabric store. This year DM's tulle has tiny golden polka dots woven into the fabric. I cut the tulle to slightly larger than both openings, and just before I need to turn on cabin lights I press it against the Velcro. Try it. Press it on at night, pull it gently off in the morning. Press on, Pull off. Repeat. Trust me. Then it's time for sleep. No matter how hot it gets during the day, it cools off at night in the Delta.

Georgiana Anchorage to Walnut Grove 11:07 – 12:07 .87 nm

5.21.20 Down with the sun, up with the roosters on a farm just the other side of the levee road. Tractors trundling by on the levee road wake me up early. Early in the morning, anchored in Georgiana Slough aboard Dura Mater: This is my kind of happy place.

Feeling down right confident about my anchoring prowess, I decide to time myself raising anchor. To be honest, the water is calm, and the wind? Well, there is no wind. Nonetheless, raising both anchors only takes me 22 minutes. There is mud everywhere but we are off the hook by 11:07.

The plan for today is to motor under the Georgiana Slough Bridge to Walnut Grove, where I plan to tie up at the pier there. Then I'll walk across the bridge to the Central Market for groceries. I plan to walk back over and down the other side of the levee road to Tony's Place. Thank you to Bill Wells, who told me that Tony's is a place where people like to talk to each other. I like talking with people and Bill says the food is good, too.

Dura Mater and I motor up and through the Georgiana Slough Bridge. The Walnut Grove Bridge operator sees Dura Mater and me coming and hails us on channel 9:

"Sailboat, do you want me to raise this bridge for you?"

Those bridge operators: They can be solicitous. I thank him and say, “Not yet. Thank you! I'll tie up at the fishing pier over this side and buy groceries first.”

I tie up at the fishing pier and climb the stairs to River Road. On the way across the bridge I stop by to say hello to James Whitaker, with whom I had such a nice chat in 2019. Mark is the bridge operator today, and it turns out James has retired and is visiting his children in Arizona. I ask Mark to give James my regards and he assures me that he will do that. I am mindful of my promise to give James a copy of this book. It's a good thing I asked for his address when I had the chance.

Over at the Central Market I replenish my pantry with two more cans of chicken noodle soup and a snickers bar for dessert. After that I mosey on back across the bridge to the Big Store and ask the proprietor if they have any garlic. I'm out of garlic, which wards off vampires and Delta pythons. He is very helpful, goes right into the back storeroom for two cloves of garlic for me. I buy that and a bag of pistachios. Garlic to keep the vampires away, pistachios just for the fun of it.

Then I walk down the hill to Tony's restaurant. It's a dark, old fashioned tavern and it's air conditioned. I order a steak sandwich from the fella behind the bar. His name is Cary. “Like the actor Cary Grant”, he tells me. Cary is the proprietor, and he is very happy that the business is able sell food again, albeit take-out only.

Earlier in the year, while closed during the pandemic, he had painted the whole place inside and refinished the bar himself. It is beautiful pressed tin covered in a clear epoxy.

Tony's Place, Walnut Grove

While waiting for my steak sandwich and onion rings I sit on the covered outdoor patio out back and drink a tall glass of iced tea. I eavesdrop on two men at the next table. Apparently CoVid swept through the Delta earlier this year during January and February. People sitting at tables six feet apart contribute to the public conversation. Everyone seems to be a local and everyone had either been sick or knew someone who had been sick with respiratory issues. They all thought it had been the flu and maybe they were right.

Walnut Grove to Steamboat Slough

052120 After eating part of my steak sandwich and taking the rest away in a box, I walked back across the highway to where Dura Mater was tied up at Deacon's Landing. After raising her sail at the dock we were under the Walnut Grove bridge @ 2:20 pm.

At first I think that our pretty bumblebee drifter will work in the conditions and it's so easy to raise. I was hopeful that we could sail close hulled with the drifter sheeted in tight, but then we turn the corner to port and the wind is right on our nose. The old Sacramento River is wide and open just past Walnut Grove, with rip rap and no trees to block the considerable wind today. So down came the drifter and on again came our Engine by Dave.

Today there is no dilly dallying. Dura Mater and I motor straight up river to the Steamboat Slough Bridge and call ahead on the radio. Demi Stewart is the bridge operator today and as she raises it for us she announces:

“The bridge opens until 10 pm! And there is no toll!"

Just below the bridge and around the first bend in Steamboat Slough we are in the same anchorage as we were in 2019, albeit with no other boats this year. Even though there is no one to admire my prowess I pivot around and accomplish another splendid job anchoring. Into the ebb.

Tightly tucked up against the tall shrubs on the west side of the slough, I cut up my tender and delicious steak from Tony’s restaurant. I cook it in olive oil with red onions, garlic and mushrooms. It’s cool and beautiful this evening, with a crystal clear sky and the sounds of insects everywhere around us.

5.22.20 The next morning I wake again to the sound of trucks pulling farm equipment close by and above us on the levee road. Accustomed to raising my sail at the dock, I make the mistake of doing so again this morning. Pulling in my stern anchor first, I move forward to raise the bow anchor. As soon as I do so the ebb is strong enough to pull DM’s bow around and down Steamboat.

Like a horse fighting the bridle, DM starts the day going sideways down the slough. It sure is a good thing that Steamboat is all muddy banks around the edges because we lurch and bump along each side in turn before I can get back to the tiller, ducking the boom twice as it gybes back and forth..

That wind up there at the top of your mast? It's not the same as the wind at water level. My editor has informed me that the appropriate nautical term for this phenomena is "wind sheer". If you're a San Francisco Bay sailor feeling nostalgic for strong consistent wind, well you're not going to get satisfaction along Steamboat Slough. There are just too many tall trees and it curves around and around, which changes everything in the sailing equation. Steamboat Slough is beautiful above Cache Slough, but below that the trees have been replaced with rip rap most of the way to the Sacramento deep water channel.

Back in 2017, as part of my initial foray into the Delta, I had called Bill Wells at the Delta Chamber of Commerce. He sent me a thick packet of laminated maps of the Delta, one of which was that fishing map that had been utterly useless to me when I first arrived by car. However, our phone conversation included the story of his own first trip from Sausalito to a place called Arrowhead Harbor. I had enjoyed Bill's description of the marina and especially his stories about his friendship with Jack Foutz, the owner of Arrowhead.

Bill told me it is not easy to find Arrowhead Harbor by car because it is "way out there in the fields". When I looked it up on the map it appeared just east of the Sacramento deep water channel, and north of the Ryer Island Ranch. Ah, yes. It looked hard to find, alright. But maybe not so hard to find by water? This was particularly appealing to me, so I called Jack Foutz. I had to drop Bill's name in order for him to pay attention, so I mentioned Bill. That did the trick.

Jack assured me that Miner Slough is deep enough for my sailboat's 4.5' draft and that there is no commercial traffic. He told me that Miner Slough is travelled only by fishermen and monitored by the marine patrol. He hadn't seen a sailboat on Miner Slough for awhile. He informed me that soundings had been taken and Miner Slough Bridge is slated for replacement. He also told me that Arrowhead Marina was being dredged for the first time in fifteen years. Mr Foutz agreed to be interviewed but asked that I call ahead for a convenient time first. He has a lot going on, he informed me.

That conversation was in 2017 and I have thought about Miner Slough ever since. On my way down to the Sacramento I stopped off at Snug Harbor, on the lower part of Steamboat Slough. Dura Mater and I parked behind a big, powerful looking Sheriff's boat, then I walked up to the little office/mini mart.

I asked about tying up for the night at the long guest dock. It would cost $35/night, but there is no fuel, no shore power and no water. I asked about cream for my coffee, but Snug Harbor doesn't sell coffee cream. I bought two cans of Diet Coke instead, then walked back down to the boat ramp. I decided to chat up the sheriff deputies.

I asked them about Miner Slough, whether it would be passable in my boat.

"Well, there's the bridge," one of them told me.

I nodded. The Miner Slough bridge requires twelve hours' notice for opening. I imagined their reckoning as they turned to evaluate Dura Mater's beautiful physical qualities.

"What do you draw? Four, five feet?" asked another sheriff.

I nodded again. They looked at each other, trying to decide something.

"There's plenty of water in there," they all agreed. They also told me that Miner Slough is on their patrol route: they might motor by during the night and check on me. Did I have an anchor light? Of course I did, I assured them. And it would be turned on.

The deputies were proud of their own boat, too. I asked for permission before stepping aboard to admire its cabin. It reminded me of the interior of a serious ocean racing sailboat: spare of comfort but with impressively powerful electronics. It also had two 300 horsepower outboard engines. It's probably not a good idea to be a criminal around these waterways.

Then I stepped aboard Dura Mater and we were on our way, in search of what would become my very favorite anchorage.

DELTA MARINA

5. 22.20 Before heading up to Miner Slough, Dura Mater and I sailed under the Rio Vista Bridge and spent the night in Delta Marina. We needed to refresh and recuperate. For $27 I gained access to a hot shower, fresh water and shore

power so I could re-charge all my gadgets: batteries for my handheld garmin, my little waterproof speaker for music and my disposable boat laptop. I call it disposable because it cost less than $150 and I bought it with the idea that I would surely drop it in the water, lose it or wreck it like I do sunglasses. Amazingly, it has lasted for longer than any pair of sunglasses I've ever owned.

The people at Delta Marina are very nice and they didn't seem to have much business this year, so I spent some money on tchotchkes in order to support the well stocked market there. I'd like to help Delta businesses stay open. Unfortunately the Point restaurant was closed this visit, but I had provisions: cans of Staag Silverado chili, heat-softened Havarti cheese and very soft chocolate for dessert. I filled up my water bottles and the next morning we were ready for adventure.

Above the Rio Vista bridge the Sacramento River branches off and becomes, essentially, two Sacramento Rivers. There is the old Sacramento branching east, and then there is the Sacramento River/ deep water channel, directly ahead, where all the freighters and fuel tankers continue north. The old Sacramento separates just below Georgiana Slough, and goes up toward Walnut Grove, to Courtland, Clarksburg and all the way to West Sacramento. I am told that sailboats can't go further than the bridge just beyond Old Sacramento.

DM and I have only gone north as far as Steamboat Slough, but other people might tell you about going further north. The wind was directly on the bow both times we've gone up river out of Walnut Grove. Your experience may differ but your mileage probably won't.

Above Walnut Grove Old Sacramento is wide enough to tack back and forth, but like most water in the Delta, it's more often ebbing than flooding. The current is strong and there are levee roads on either side, with River Road on the one side, Highway 160 on the other, and few trees alongside, so if there's wind it can be powerful with gusts.

Dura Mater and I left Delta Marina at 7:39 am and motorsailed up the Sacramento River. Once under the Rio Vista Bridge I turned off the engine and unfurled her working jib. We got big wind and it was exhilarating until we got stuck between the old Sacramento and the Steamboat Slough entrance, where the water swirled around as the tides merged and changed, creating eddies impressive enough so that I turned on DM's Engine by Dave. Then we continued up the River.

By 9:23 am the water had smoothed out, and we were able to make wide tacks up river. That was easy because the Sacramento River is really wide in here. We continued on until we reached Cache Slough and further up, Prospect Slough. I had read that article by LaDonna Buback about Prospect Slough and I was determined to see it.

Prospect Slough

The sky was blue and fields spread out on all sides. The water was full of purposeful fishermen steering their silent trolling motors with their feet. There was significant current and the wind was strong on this day, due to the fetch across the expanse of water to our left.

Liberty Island, flooded more than ten years earlier, is no longer an island, but an open area where wind is not checked by trees. Up ahead marker #53 on the river could be clearly seen from inside Prospect Slough. Keeping an eye on the depth finder, as it became shallower DM and I pivoted around.

A huge ship seemed to be plowing through the fields toward Sacramento. It rose above a low row of tule islands, moving powerfully along just yards the other side of the tall grasses. Those big ships? They can be quiet and sneak up on you and there are no traffic lights out here. As we exited into the Sacramento River I looked carefully both ways, then scootched across to the opening of Miner Slough.

Rio Vista Bridge to Miner Slough Bridge 11.23 nm

Just above the entrance to Miner Slough hundreds of herons and other birds are walking around in a wide muddy flat area. Now, I know better than to sail over to where birds are walking on water, but my chart plotter suggests that the entrance is close by, through a narrow space in the tules. So we take a chance and sail slowly through. Very slowly.

Miner Slough

Once past the birds in the mud to port and through the narrow space we are in bulrush territory and it is unbelievably beautiful and quiet and empty. Except for that fella fishing over there with his wife, and those two over there in their camouflage jackets, and those two boats over there in the shallower water, all of them waiting quietly and patiently for fish to get tricked onto their hooks with their shiny lures. We glide by and no one pays us any attention.

Miner Slough curves around and around, with trees and shrubs along its length all the way to the pretty little Miner Slough Bridge. The depth is more than adequate all along, averaging 32' rather than the 28' indicated by the chart plotter. The deepest spot is 45' and the only shallow spot is at the curve in the slough just outside Arrowhead Harbor, where it is 16'... 15'... 14' ...

Arrowhead is really tucked away in here. There is a bridge that needs painting, the pilings might or might not be rotting, and it appears to be silted in too much for a keel boat. In other words, it is a "lost isle" type of place that is very appealing to a certain kind of ... what did Rob Tryon call it ... a river rat? It is appealing to me, for sure.

I call the office by cell phone and identify myself. Could I speak with Jack Foutz? I am informed that Mr Foutz is too busy to talk with me and NO! We should definitely not try to come into the harbor in a sailboat! It is only two feet deep in there!

So we don't.

Instead Dura Mater and I continue along the winding Miner Slough, motor sailing slowly now, meandering past any number of muddy beaches with no overhanging trees that might interfere with our rigging. There are several ideal places for us to anchor along the way, and when we get to the bridge we stop and do just that. The Miner Slough Bridge requires 12 hour notice for opening, but we don't want to go any further today, anyway.

If I had a dinghy I could row in for ice and whatever else Jack Foutz has on offer. But I don't. The sun is going down and I have decided that Miner Slough is my favorite anchorage of all in the Delta. I wonder whether I should delete all this information or leave it here? What if, upon my return, I find Miner Slough clogged with enormous catamarans and cabin cruisers with propane generators running air conditioning late into the night? Those fishermen? They will not be pleased with me. If you are reading this, let it be our little secret, okay?

Miner Slough Bridge

Our evening anchored in Miner Slough is utterly quiet. Not one vehicle crosses the bridge the whole time. A few fishing boats motor by as the sun sets, pausing to look at Dura Mater where she faces the bridge, anchored bow and stern. This is small motorboat territory.

5.22.20 After spending our last night of the year in the Delta, it is now 5 am. It is the highest tide of the day at 4.3' above low tide and the slough is still flooding. DM was held securely in place during the night by two anchors: a Danforth at the front and a big spade anchor at the stern. To be fair, we would only have needed tiny anchors at each end, but they were the anchors at hand.

Meanwhile we're floating pleasantly here on the water and I watch as the sun comes up and fishermen mosey on by.

Breakfast aboard Dura Mater

We wave and smile at each other. The slough isn't wide and they pass by very close. It's Memorial Day weekend and they're on their own boats, too. We're all happy here.

I decide that it is time for us to head home so I put the breakfast dishes in the sink. No sense in ruining a perfectly good morning by washing dirty dishes. First things first: I let the stern line out and sit on the bow while I slowly pull Dura Mater forward toward the Danforth at the bow. It comes up clean, and I lay it on top of the 50' of rode and 30' of chain. Yes, maybe that was overly cautious of me. Better safe than sorry. If there had been a tsunami we would have remained safely anchored.

Then I go back to collect the plow anchor at the stern, but it won't budge. We are well and truly stern anchored. I remind myself that it is a lovely morning, take a breath and go below to make a small pot of coffee. I don't plan on being here forever and caffeine assists with the sense of urgency. Then I sit in the cockpit and cogitate the state of being stuck in a beautiful place while I drink it. I feel like an unsupervised child. This is not anything to worry about, I think to myself. Eventually, though, that anchor must be gotten.

I finish my coffee, add all that paraphernalia to the pile in the sink, and turn to the issue at hand. I try to winch up the damned anchor. No chance. I turn on the Engine by Dave and try to pull it out by motoring forward, tugging gently. It's not going to happen. I think about my options. Maybe I can free dive into that murky water. I do have a pair of swimming goggles. However, the anchor is in 16' of water and my maximum breath- holding ability is about equal to the depth of a nice, clean swimming pool. And besides, there are big fish in that water. I've seen them. And there might be pythons, too.

So I cogitate some more and open a can of ready-made Starbucks espresso with cream. These are for emergencies.

What would a real sailor do? Well, a real sailor would never leave an expensive anchor behind. I throw the empty coffee can into DM's galley. Rob told me that stern anchoring is all about scope. I have more scope. Of course I have more scope! Never throw out anything that cost money, that's my motto. I might need it one day.

The ebb has started now. I attach many more feet of scope to the anchor line and we motor slowly forward until we're almost at the bridge. We've got scope! Then Dura Mater and I turn into the slowly building ebb with her magnificent new Schumacher rudder and can sneak the entrenched anchor from behind. Yes, we do. And even though it is powerfully dug into our own private little mud beach, our tug from the rear results in – success! That anchor just gives it up! What a grand anchor! I love this anchor! Finally, finally, as I drag it behind us to rinse off all that wonderful, dirty mud, we can begin to head slowly back to the deep water channel of the Sacramento River through all the delicious twists and turns of Miner Slough.

Delta Marina to Benicia Marina: 31.45 nm. Left at 7:30 am, arrived @ 11:55 am.

On May 23, 2020, Dura Mater and I exited Miner Slough. Motorsailing under the Rio Vista Bridge and past Delta Marina, the ebb carried us all the way down the Sacramento River to Benicia Marina. We experienced no big wind, no square waves. It was a remarkably uneventful return trip compared to those in all three previous years. It was a different time of year, of course, early summer instead of late, and it took us only 4 hours 15 minutes.

Our moving average was 7.4 knots, maximum speed 10.7 knots. We checked into Benicia Marina @ 11:55 am and settled into slip 47. I walked into into town, ordered a large latte and a Greek Salad. After eating that in the sunshine outside the cafe I returned to the Marina and took a shower. We were back in civilization. I wasn't sure how I felt about that.

The sun has gone down. It's time to go to sleep in Dura Mater's v berth for the last time during this trip, and I am all done writing for now.

EXPLANATIONS AND EXCUSES

Caveat: a warning enjoining one from certain acts or practices; an explanation to prevent misinterpretation (Webster's Ninth New Collegiate Dictionary, 1988).

Many people have spent more time in the California Delta than I have. The magazine ***Latitude 38*** has published stories about people sailing in the Delta since August of 1977 and the ***Bay & Delta Yachtsman*** has been covering the Delta boating scene for the same number of years. I have been told that whole generations of families have spent year after year together there on one kind of boat or another.

This book is a sort of travelogue, a series of snapshots of my own time spent there on my sailboat over the course of four summers. Looking back, my intentions were so uncomplicated! I would simply write about my experiences camper/sailing in the Delta. Writing about the places I sail to on Dura Mater is my way of sharing the experience. Because I sail alone. Or solo. Singlehanded is the word. That doesn't mean sailing with only one hand. It's the definition of a person who sails without anyone else on the boat.

People ask why I sail alone. For me, sailing alone is like coloring outside the lines. I don't have to ask permission and I get to make all the decisions. The problem solving is satisfying and the mistakes are all mine. Singlehanded sailing makes me feel like a child without adult supervision.

When I arrived in the California Delta aboard my boat Dura Mater in July of 2017 I was stunned by the heat. During the summer months it is hot everywhere in the Delta, and a good thing, too. Because the Delta is where an enormous amount of farming occurs. Dirt + sunshine + heat + hard labor by farmers = food enjoyed by people who live in every state in America.

The crops that are grown here, the goats and cattle, the eggs laid by the chickens and the fruit trees that stretch as far as you can see into the distance are only one hour away from my home in urban Oakland. The food grown in the Delta's rich soil, quenched by the miles of waterways that run through it, provides sustenance to people around the world.

When I drive back and forth to my boat from Oakland to the Sacramento Delta, I take Highway 24, then 680 toward Sacramento. After twenty minutes I turn off onto 242 until the sign says "Antioch Bridge" and then I'm driving up and over the San Joaquin River, where the landscape is completely - and I mean COMPLETELY - different.

When I get to the top of that one lane bridge and look out over the rich farmland of the Delta, with the wind generators in the distance and the wide ribbons of water on either side of the highway, my whole body relaxes. I'm heading to a very different place, a slower one, a perfect way to live under the radar.

Every year when I sail under the Antioch Bridge from the Bay Area I am astonished again at the stark difference between the factories on this side of the Bridge and the farmland that side of it. Descending from the urbanity of the San Francisco Bay Area into the farmland itself from the top of the Antioch Bridge offers the same dissonance: It is like travelling from Outside to Over There.

Over the four summers I spent in the California Delta I learned to just give myself up to it. And once I'd done that, I came to realize that directions didn't really matter. Because the Delta means something different to each person, and how they get there isn't determined by roads or waterways. The California Delta is a state of mind.

REFERENCES AND RESOURCES

Buback, LaDonna. Prospect Slough, 2011, also in Latitude 38, Lush Life in the Delta, June 2011. This is a terrific article filled with local knowledge. It can be found here: http://www.deltadoodah.com/articles/LushLife.html

Eberling, Barry, October 27, 2013 Solano County: Rio Vista Bridge Tender has Million-dollar View The Daily Republic, Solano County's news source

Eckblom, Frank R, 1975 On the Delta: Action Guide II. Thank you to Dave Cowell, s/v Mas Tiempo, for this publication.

Fimrite, Peter. Delta residents vent about Jerry Brown's twin tunnels water plan San Francisco Chronicle, November 30, 2017

Gardner, Erle Stanley. The World of Water: ExpLoreng the Sacramento Delta. New York, N.Y. William Morrow & Company, 1964.

Gardner, Erle Stanley. Drifting Down the Delta. New York, N.Y. William Morrow & Company, 1969.

Jensen, Carol A. The California Delta, 2007, Arcadia Publishing. Hal Schell archives ; East Contra Costa Historical Society.

Nomellini, Dante J. Central Delta Water Agency's Comments on the "Notice of Preparation of Environmental Impact Report for the Delta Conveyance Project", April 17, 2020.

Over Troubled Waters, UTube video, 2015: https://www.youtube.com/watch?v=060jEwexRoo

Schell, Hal. Dawdling on the Delta: The Complete Cruising Guide for California's Fabulous 1,000-Mile Delta. Stockton, California: Schell Books, 1983.

Swagerty, W.R. and Smith, Reuben W. Stitching a River Culture: Trade, Communication and Transportation to 1960. An essay of The Delta Narratives Project, Delta Protection Commission, State of California. June 1, 2015.

United States Coast Pilot 7: 2020 (52nd) Edition. Pacific Coast: California. National Oceanic and Atmospheric Administration.

Walters, Bob. Cruising the California Delta II. Newfoundland, New Jersey: Haessner Publishing, 1976.

Zaremba, L. & Carroll, J. Summer Wind Flow Regimes over the Sacramento Valley, American Meteorology Society, October 1999.

Latitude 38 everything Delta Doo Dah.

Photo book: Mandeville Island: A Fine Balance 2005 Tuscany Research Institute.

Locke and the Sacramento Delta Chinatowns, 2013 Lawrence Tom, Brian Tom, and the Chinese American Museum of Northern California. Arcadia Publishing. Atmospheric Science Section, Department of Land, Air, and Water Resources, University of California, Davis

PHOTOGRAPHS

All the photographs in this book are mine except for the photograph of Tom Patterson's daughter, Stephanie and Bill Wells' photograph of his boat, Ranger. I took hundreds and hundreds of color photos because I just couldn't get enough of the beauty of the places I visited. The photographs for this book were chosen because they readily converted from color to greyscale, which is what kept this book from being more expensive.

Color versions of these and more photographs and Delta stories can be found online at the forum for the Singlehanded Sailing Society https://www.sfbaysss.org/forum/forum.php.

Look for the threads: **Sailing Tomorrow** and **What I Saw**.

A LIST OF DELTA NECESSITIES

plastic clothespins
beach umbrella
lightweight cloth to use as bimini
easy food
mosquito netting: aka tulle and narrow sticky back Velcro
bug lotion: whatever works
raft, paddles, foot pump
rechargeable batteries, charging cords for laptop, phone
portable rechargeable power blocks
fresh water: lots of it
books, music, Bluetooth speaker
shore power cord
extra anchor
extra line: Lots of it
diesel
bathing suit, towel, flip flops
coffee
mio or similar for water
sunglasses and sunhats
zinc oxide sticks, sunblock, lots of it
dawn dishsoap
notebooks and lots of pens
camera or video

INTERVIEWS

ACKNOWLEDGEMENTS

My very first interview in the California Delta was with Mr and Mrs French, who so very kindly sat down at the picnic bench with me at B&W's beach where they were congregated with their extended family members. That was in 2017.

Thank you to Christine Weaver, Delta Doodette, for luring me up the Delta. I wouldn't have gone there if I hadn't trusted her judgement.

During four summers Owl Harbor served as my mother ship. Devery Stockon fed me vegetables, eggs and Curtis's garlic. Devery was unendingly patient, gracious and warm. During the great pandemic of 2020, while my local public library was closed, I was able to borrow books from Devery's library. They fed my essential need for written words.

No matter where I go in the Delta, people ask me if I've read Hal Schell's books. Yes! Before my first visit I had already read **Dawdling on the Delta** cover to cover. I also read Delta books by Bob Walters and Erle Stanley Gardner.

The San Joaquin is clogged with sailboats during the annual Delta Ditch Run race from Richmond to Stockton, but most of those boats disperse and return to the San Francisco Bay right after the race. Many are towed home by trailer and some of them even head up into the mountains where they race each other around Lake Tahoe for the rest of the summer. Except for our participation in the Delta Doo Dah, during visits to the Delta Dura Mater and I found very few sailboats.

Some of the marinas Schell wrote about are gone now, and you can't rent a houseboat anywhere. That's a shame because I think more people would enjoy dawdling somewhere on the water without "tipping sideways" as non-sailors refer to the heeling intrinsic to sailboats.

I found Hal Schell's Delta reflected still in the people who live there today. As I spent time in the Delta I became intrigued, as was Schell, by the culture of the place. Driving from Oakland to the Delta takes less than an hour (without traffic), and then you enter a whole different world.

The namesake for my Engine by Dave, Dave Morris can fix anything and improves everything else along the way. Almost ten years ago Dave diagnosed an issue with Dura Mater's engine that had eluded everyone else. Then he fixed it from the inside out and put it back together again. I am still grateful today.

Thank you to my two friends and editors, Skip Allan and Bob Johnston. Both fine sailors and writers themselves, they read proofs of this book and corrected most of my egregious mistakes. All errors or wrong-headed opinions are mine alone.

Thank you to everyone who shared your Delta story with me. If I have forgotten to thank you, I apologize.

When I need some item for Dura Mater I can always count on my son to buy it for me. I simply text a photo to him and it shows up on my doorstep. My darling boy, Max has the uncanny ability to phone me when I am sailing in heavy wind. When I tell him so, his response is unfailingly upbeat: "Of course you are, Mama!"

Finally, thank you to the Voice of Reason, who set up a discrete corner of an upstairs room with a desk, a lamp and a rug. I pinned all my Delta maps to a corkboard on the wall behind my chair.

Then I wrote this book.

1, 22: 22

Thanks again, Tom: for the coffee, for the pastries, for all our lovely conversations about boats.

jackie